CRIME & REASON:
A BLACK CHOICE

An introduction to the birth of black on black crime and social dysfunction

Marques Lowery

iUniverse®

CRIME & REASON: A BLACK CHOICE
AN INTRODUCTION TO THE BIRTH OF BLACK ON BLACK
CRIME AND SOCIAL DYSFUNCTION

iUniverse books may be ordered through booksellers or by contacting:

iUniverse
1663 Liberty Drive
Bloomington, IN 47403
www.iuniverse.com
844-349-9409

ISBN: 978-1-5320-8417-1 (sc)
ISBN: 978-1-5320-8418-8 (e)

Library of Congress Control Number: 2019914787

Print information available on the last page.

iUniverse rev. date: 09/23/2022

Chapter Outline

Introduction Institutional Racism 1

Chapter 1   Political concepts that created racism..5

Chapter 2   "The Color of Racism" 8

Chapter 3   Politics & Racism 12

Chapter 4   Birth of a Nation..18

Chapter 5   The Birth of White Privilege 24

Chapter 6   Introduction into Black Consciousness. 28

Chapter 7   Part 1: The Emergence of the New Negro 31

Chapter 8   Understanding Double Consciousness: Social Dilemma's 35

Chapter 9   The Importance of Self-Consciousness...39

Chapter 10   Developmental Psychology...43

Chapter 11   Cracks in the pavement...53

Chapter 12   social programming, the calm before the storm...................................58

Chapter 13   Triple stages of darkness 61

Chapter 14   Part one: the 50's..63

Chapter 15   Part 2: Civil rights movement 66

Chapter 16   Riots and Radicals 71

Chapter 17   Part 3: the birth of the sub-cultural influence 1965-1975 75

Chapter 18   Part 4: sub-cultural effect..78

Chapter 19   part 5: warring ideology 82

Chapter 20   Malcolm X Vs. El Hajj Malik Shabbazz...102

Chapter 21   Christianity vs Islam 107

Chapter 22   Part 1 Religion and Indoctrination 110

Chapter 23 124

Chapter 24   Social movement...130

Chapter 25 133

Chapter 26 138

Chapter 27 143

Chapter 28 culture shift.. 149

Chapter 29 154

Chapter 30 157

Chapter 31 163

Chapter 32 black on black crime and its origin.. 167

Chapter 33 anatomy of violence 169

Chapter 34 Here is something to analyze 175

Chapter 35 War on Minorities 178

Chapter 36 Three Strikes Laws... 179

Chapter 37 183

Chapter 38 184

Chapter 39 capitalism... 187

Chapter 40 Part 1: Psychological Perspectives & Social Norms 189

Chapter 41 191

Chapter 42 social institutes that govern the world 193

Chapter 43 Individualistic Vs collectivistic culture 196

Chapter 44 Multitude of social groups /rap music gangs /individualistic culture............. 198

Chapter 45 Socially Constructed Environments Began to Ignite Social Stress That

Later Contributed To Mental Disorders.. 201

Chapter 46 Separation Amongst the Group 204

The savage repression of blacks, which can be estimated by reading the obituary columns of the nation's dailies, Fred Hampton, etc., has not failed to register on the black inmates.

<u>George Jackson</u>

"You have to understand that people have to pay the price for peace. You dare to struggle, you dare to win. If you dare not struggle, then goddammit you don't deserve to win.``"You have to understand that people have to pay the price for peace. You dare to struggle, you dare to win.

"The process of empowerment cannot be simplistically defined in accordance with our own particular class interests. We must learn to lift as we climb." – Angela Davis"

CRIME & REASON: A BLACK CHOICE

The purpose of this book

Crime and Reason, a Black Choice. What does it mean to the average person reading this book? What does the text entail, is it based on formulating practices of accountability more so then, victims of circumstances. Some may question the stance on this book, and may not agree with some of the text. This book focuses on issues that have plagued black America for over 400 years. The institutional racism embedded in the 6 major social institutes that govern society affect blacks more than any other group in America. From the slaves boats that hovered Africa, right to the shores of South Carolina, blacks have been at the foot of white America. The psychological component associated with the nature of slavery, and The repression of ones freedom trangress into generational depression, pyschological oppression and inferority has become a genetic component. This inferiority has affected the current generation and has contributed to high crimes against one another. Prior to 1970's, blacks were deprived the right to live as a human, and were subjected to physical abuse by whites, police, and the KKK, along with deprived access into social institutions. To understand the dynamics of blacks, is to understand America to its totality. Unfortunately today, blacks are faced with the same racist element from the past. However, the increase in crime associated with blacks are the result of choices, and not social inequality. What is social inequality? Social inequality is slavery, Jim Crow laws, Black wall street, Black codes, and KKK. Today, blacks have access to vote, own homes, attend prestigious colleges, own business, obtain bank loans, political positions, senators, and a president. Blacks from 1619-1954, did not have the same freedom, and access as the current generation, giving the title Crime and Reason a Black Choice.

INTRODUCTION

INSTITUTIONAL RACISM

The savage repression of blacks, which can be estimated by reading the obituary columns of the nation's dailies, Fred Hampton, etc., has not failed to register on the black inmates.

George Jackson

Society is governed by social institutes that develop the complexity of the world. This complexity shapes the cultural perspectives, and status of an individual or group. This complexity shapes and mold politics, and ideologies that influence the masses. The five major social institutions in sociology are family, education, religion, government (political), and the economy. Institutional racism is racism that discriminates, negates the advancement of a particular group, and embed discriminatory policies that advance the systemic racism that permeates future generations. Discrimination or unequal treatment on the basis of membership in a particular ethnic group (typically one that is a minority or marginalized), arising from systems, structures, or expectations that have become established within an institution or organization. Institutional racism is the generalized discrimination against an entire racial group that has been incorporated into a public or social system, like the criminal justice system, public education, health care, or even private institutions like ivy league universities or professional organizations. To understand institutional racism, is to understand slavery in its totality. The Africans that arrived were products of trade agreements, therefore, they would be subjected to institutional racism to maintain two social institutes (politics and economy). The first stage of institutional racism implemented was religion. Religion, was forced upon slaves to create a narriative that would indoctrinate them. The religious indocrination would be forced upon african slaves, and by the 1800's, this indocrtination had become the infrastructure of black

1

families. By 1808, the african slave trade was abolished. Once the slave trade seized, africa in the americas lost all ties to there ancestry. By the end of the 1800's, the generation at that moment would have lost all connection to its roots, and this would develop the institutional racism that perpetuates present social institutes. Slavery, which was governed by politics, and econmic advancement for white americans, denied african american equal opportunity in education, health care, and econmic opportunites. The denial of economic advancement affects the family structure.

What is racism, and how does it affect the minority, or the marginalized ethnic group? Racism in America will exist as long as the social institutions that govern the world are entrenched in racist ideologies. The American (1)economy was established off the degradation of another human being, which in return, developed racism. The organizations and families that profited, help develop laws and policies to keep african american in a caste system. A growing body of research shows that centuries of racism in this country has had a profound and negative impact on communities of color. "The impact is pervasive and deeply embedded in our society—affecting where one lives, learns, works, worships and plays and creating inequities in access to a range of social and economic benefits—such as housing, education, wealth, and employment. CDC.gov(2011)

How does institutional racism from the past evolve to the present day 2020's?

Between 2013-2021, there have been 2,391 police killings of African American men. https://www.statista.com/statistics/1124036/number-people-killed-police-ethnicity-us/.

Within this time frame, Mississippi killed 51, Alabama 62, Georgia 108, Florida 179, Missouri 74, Texas 167, North Carolina 87, Maryland 90, New Jersey 61, New York 81, Pennsylvania 68, Virginia 62, Ohio 90, California 196, and Louisiana 90.

Number of executions by lynching in the United States by state and race between 1882 and 1968

within this 86 year time frame, 3,065 people of color was lynched. Mississippi lynched 539, Alabama 299, georgia 492, florida 257, Texas 352, North carolina 86, maryland 27, New Jersey 1, New York 1, Pennsylvania 6, Virginia 83, California 2, and louisiana 335.

When we look at racist states of the past that had a high number of lynching, we can see they have a high number of police killing of blacks.

Mississippi lynched 539, police killed 61 between 2013-2021, Goergia lynched 492, police killed 108, Texas lynched 352, police killed, Alabama lynched 299, police killed 62. On average, police killings happen more than lynchinging. The states with the most lynching, and police killing are highly operated by Klansmen, who are government official, prosecutors, police officers, senators, and governors. Each of the above mentioned plays a vital role in the criminal justice system.

"The ten states with the highest prison populations in the country are Texas (154,749), California (122,417), Florida (96,009), Georgia (54,113), Ohio (50,338), Pennsylvania (45,485), New York (43,439), Arizona (40,951), Illinois (38,259), and Michigan (38,053). In terms of imprisonment rate per 100,000 people, Louisiana, Oklahoma, and Mississippi have the highest rates, 680, 639, and 636, respectively." https://worldpopulationreview.com/ state-rankings/prison-population-by-state

Institutional racism is woven into the infrastructure of America. Slavery helped establish the country economic and political position in the world, the same organizations and families that controlled the slave trade, control the instituiton, and this is one way the institutional racism from the past evolved to the present. Would that make racism biological, genetic, or environmental, or all three.

You can tell the tree by the fruit it bears. You see it through what the organization is delivering as far as a concrete program. If the tree's fruit sours or grows brackish, then the time has come to chop it down - bury it and walk over it and plant new seeds.

Huey Newton

Chapter 1

Political concepts that created racism

Racism is taught in our society; it is not automatic. It is learned behavior toward persons with dissimilar physical characteristics.

Alex Haley

Racism, what is it, and what does it represent? Is racism a disease? and if not dealt with, does it permeate for generations, causing a genetic predisposition within the family. A genetic predisposition is a genetic characteristic which influences the possible phenotypic development of an individual organism within a species or population under the influence of environmental conditions. A phenotype is the set of observable characteristics of an individual resulting from the interaction of its genotype with the environment. Psychologists have concurred multiple twin studies which define the effect of genetic predisposition, and behavioral genetics (Schuetze, S. 2013). Most studies were conducted to determine behavior based on genetic predisposition. Henry, J.Dionne, G.,Viding, E.,Petitclerc, A.,Feng, B.,Vitaro, F., Boivin, M. (2018). The understanding of this psychological term gives insight to racism, and overt racism as a genetic predisposition passed down through the lineage. As we understand the concept of phenotypic behavior, we concur that its an observable behavior, resulting from interaction with the environment. Meaning, if homes pass down their racist ideologies, and definition of blacks, it will in return become the perception of the offspring. Although overt racism still adversely affects the well-being and advancement of Black Americans, subtle racism also has a pervasive influence. Color-blind racism, a form of subtle racism, rationalizes the current disadvantaged status of Black Americans and institutionalized practices that perpetuates the disadvantage. The present article, adopting a psychological perspective, reviews the evidence on the existence and dynamics of contemporary forms of color-blind racism. Dovidio J.F., Gaertner, S.L.,&Saguy, T. (2015). Racism does not start with the present generation, the ideologies, and concepts that permeate the family are generational, and taught. Example, a southern white family that has ties to the confederate, the chances of the offspring having racist views, is consistent with a generation of racist. Racism comes in many forms. These forms of racism after years governed the political and economic structure of the country. The transition went from overt racism to institutionalized racism, and systematic oppression. (Paradies, Y.2006). This oppression governed the economic structure and created systematic racism. The two racist structures that are responsible for the mindset of people becoming racist, is economic racism and structural racism. Economic racism affects black more than others. With social injustice, blacks are deferred opportunities to advance financially by way of economic racism. Racism and social injustice created an innate inferiority complex. Innate inferiority complexes distinguish from years of oppression that are genetic predisposition within African American. Structural racism is defined as, "A system in which public policies, institutional practices, cultural representations, and other norms work in various, often reinforcing ways to perpetuate racial group inequity. It identifies dimensions of our history and culture that have allowed privileges associated with "whiteness" and disadvantages associated with "color" to endure and adapt over time. Structural racism is not something that a few people or institutions choose to practice, Instead, it has been a feature of the social, economic and political systems in which we all exist." These two concepts fall under institutional racism which is practiced through social and political forums. This form of covert racism infiltrated the judicial system for 100's of years, laws and rules were created with biases toward minorities, and formulated by white America. The formulation of laws and rules that casted out other groups that were present in America eventually led to the concept of racism for generations to come. As the American economy increased with resources, so did the racism toward blacks and other minorities. Institutions began to rise but excluded from those institutions were blacks. The resources that flourished in America made way for the success of white America. As the slave trade increased, America became a country on the rise. Cheap labor allowed slave owners to save enough money to do trading. This

6

cheap labor helped the American economy grow, and do trading with other countries. The economic important of slavery undermined the humanistic perspectives. White America lacked compassion or empathy for blacks, and from there birthed the grotesque history of racism.

I've been suffering A loss of identity lately. I'm sure that you can see That the person I once was Is not currently who I am... I've been feeling slightly odd lately And I wish that I could say That I'll be over it quite quickly But I think I've lost my way... My bearings are all boggled And I've gotten all mixed up Am I really upside down... Or is it actually a downside up?? I have no wish to offend thee But surely you can see If you give me back my maple leaf I'll be as happy as can be!! Dee Daffodil (HW) 11 Sep,2007

Chapter 2

"The Color of Racism"

You can tell the tree by the fruit it bears. You see it through what the organization is delivering as far as a concrete program. If the tree's fruit sours or grows brackish, then the time has come to chop it down - bury it and walk over it and plant new seeds.

Huey Newton

Racism is a psychological element that contributes to a physiological problem. Racism has been classified as a stressor. Analyzing racism from a psychological perspective, there is a relevant physiological component. Tense arousal is defined as having a negative, and unpleasant feeling. (Schimmack & Reisenzein,2002) Tense arousal stems from evaluation anxiety during social situations. (Decker2014). Arousal causes physiological change within the body; this physiological change is related to hormone release. Other responses to tense arousal are clammy hands, butterflies in the stomach, and possible fidgeting. "the brain sends signals to the adrenal glands, which are located on top of the kidneys. The adrenal glands are responsible for the release of adrenaline and cortisol, which in return affect various organs. Adrenaline prepares the body for fight or flight response, causing the heart to pump faster, opening the air passages to the lungs to provide more oxygen to the muscles, shunting blood away from where it is not needed." (Decker2014). These responses cause physical symptoms, such as; allergies, colds, flu, headaches, neck, shoulder ache, sleep disturbance, sweating, and indigestion. (Decker2014)

African Americans feel discrimination from all walks of life except sport, this discrimination, stereotypes, and prejudices that govern the world has molded the image of African American. Distorted images, and self-inflicting conflicts caused African American to succumb to the racial element that was established for them. Understanding the physiological component associated with racism, along with the understanding of behavioral genetics, and genetic predisposition, blacks may possess an innate inferiority when dealing with White Americans, and within that innate inferiority lies psychological tension with dealing with other groups. My theory of the innate inferiority of blacks, is designed from a history of psychological abuse, social oppression, physical abuse, and lynching. This history is embedded in the souls of black folks, just as a sense of superiority, and white privilege is ingrained in some whites. Racism is a social issue that contributes to a psychological component that eventually leads to anxiety, depression, PTSD, and other co-occurring behavior that exist when alcohol and drugs are coping mechanisms. The physiological combined with the psychological creates a social dilemma that affects the African American population. As media influenced increased, racism that existed from slavery and the misrepresentation of the bible led to stereotypes, biases, and prejudices. These three social issues designed the cultural representation of African Americans to the masses. As immigrants migrated to the Americas, the racial prejudice, and stereotypes created by white American became the immigrant's perspective of blacks, no matter if they were the same complexion. By the 1800's the African culture that blacks had known in the East was now replaced with a different dialect, diet, religion, and understanding into their true ancestor's. The culture of Africa had faded, as well as the names and symbolic images that represented some religious aspect. The first stage of racism was recreating the black image and redefining the true element of beauty. The image that came from Africa was considered that of evil, wide nose, thick lips, etc was images defined as ugly and unattractive. Coarse hair was considered the lowest grade of hair. The African diet was also distorted and replaced with pork, and low-grade food. During slavery, black was giving the scraps and made soul food from it.

Black culture transformed many art forms into realistic images. With history rooted In African ancestry, African American would tap into their ancestral identification that was stripped from them over the past centuries. The beauty of this is the genetic component that would arise amongst the psychological, and physical abuse that was used to distort the image of black. Music, dancing, and overall joyfulness would still be displayed no matter the hardship. The art form was a clear representation into the time, and the struggle that was being endured. African American culture took what they had and created a culture. This culture was rich in religion, dancing, singing, poetry, writing, and inventions. Slaves used their free time to indulge in the above activities. Songs, and negro spirituals became historical songs, displaying the talent of slaves. Unfortunately, just as it has always been, blacks' culture would become exploited for monetary gains. White America utilized blacks in any form to create their own wealth, and this would soon be displayed in the 1800's. black minstrels became a popular form of entertainment. Minstrels consisted of whites, with their faces painted black mimicking slaves as entertainment. The characters that were created were mere identifications into how blacks were perceived through the eyes of white America. Blacks were ridiculed, and their culture taken for granted. This was a psychological blow that would carry on into generations to come. By the late 1850's, minstrels became large, and white began using blacks to play these roles. This became an opportunity, and blacks lined up for it. Sad to say, this was a clear representation of how white America utilizes blacks' culture to increase their income. Spiritual hymns created by slaves became common church songs. As blacks played the role of minstrel, black entertainment was soon born. The images of blacks were utilized for entertainment, and soon this became an opportunity for blacks to make money entertaining whites by degrading their image. As the degradation of the black image was made for the amusement of whites; books, plays, and music began to display blacks as savages and wanted the white woman for his prize. This distortion made black start using products that bleached their skin and straighten their hair. It would not be until1960 that black would go back to their natural roots. The racial establishment of blacks was now the opposite of white. Black represented everything opposed to white, which represented dominance.

The color barrier would invade the black population, light skin, versus dark skin became a racist Component created by white America, and this made bleaching products become popular. Dark skin blacks became envious of light skin blacks, which became a racism amongst African Americans. When we hear the word racism, we first think black and white. Racism is defined as, "prejudice, discrimination, or antagonism directed against someone of a different race based on the belief that one's own race is superior." The three components that define racism re oppressive terms that base solely on one's opinion of the other. By America being a superpower, their influence governed the world's perspective of African americans. "The importance of race is that it is a social marker of identity, allowing the identification of 'the other', and as a way of seeing people as part of collective identity groups. Racism and attacks on 'other' groups become more prominent when there is a shortage of resources, when other groups may be perceived to be a threat to self-growth and access to resources, such as employment, housing and other benefits. Yet, these views are also persistent as latent ideas and deeply held attitudes about self and other, and they are shaped by historical memories and events that define and influence modern race relations." The impact of racism on mental health. (The Synergi Collaborative Centre.(www. synergicollaborativecentre.co.uk)

And now it's winter

Winter in America

And all of the healers done been killed or sent away

Yeah, and the people know, people know

It's winter

Winter in America

And ain't nobody fighting

Cause nobody knows what to save

And ain't nobody fighting

Cause nobody knows, nobody knows

And ain't nobody fighting

Cause nobody knows what to save

Gil Scott Heron

Chapter 3

Politics & Racism

To understand how any society functions you must understand the relationship between the men and the women.

Angela Davis

How does politics govern the mentality of the world? Politics are responsible for the social climate of the world. Political agendas implement structural, and economical racism. After the civil war, the emancipation proclamation freed slaves under Lincoln presidency. "In a fundamental sense, political authority may be preserved from the threat of civil war only when there exists in the political community an agreement on the basic principles of the regime. Such a consensus is the result, among other things, of a shared "ideology" that gives fellow citizens a sense of communal belonging and recognizes interlocking values, interests, and beliefs. Ideology, in this sense, may be the product of many different forces." (D. Alan Heslop207). Unfortunately, Lincoln's assassination led to Andrew Johnson preceding Lincoln. Born in North Carolina under the confederate, Andrew sat to do away with all Lincoln was looking to establish. His history, rich in white supremacy, wasted no time establishing it. Representing the democratic party Johnson moved swiftly in catering to the confederate unions." After the 1831 Nat Turner Rebellion, Tennessee adopted a new state constitution with a provision to disenfranchise free blacks. Johnson supported the provision and campaigned around the state for its ratification, giving him wide exposure." Johnson originally opposed the Emancipation Proclamation, but after gaining an exemption for Tennessee and realizing that it was an important tool for ending the war, he accepted it. His acceptance wasn't for the sake of black folks, it was based primarily on a tool to end the war. When Congress reconvened, members expressed outrage at the president's clemency orders and his lack of protecting black civil rights. In 1866, Congress passed the Freedmen's Bureau bill, providing essentials for former slaves and protection of their rights in court. They then passed the Civil Rights Act, defining "all persons born in the United States and not subject to any foreign power, excluding Indians not taxed," as citizens. Johnson vetoed these two measures because he felt that Southern states were not represented in Congress and believed that setting suffrage policy was the responsibility of the states, not the federal government. Both vetoes were overridden by Congress.

The political racism was implemented to reestablish slavery without the physical component. After the civil war, and while Johnson was in office southern whites began to feel empowered. This empowerment created black codes.

South Carolina's Black Code applied only to "persons of color," defined as including anyone with more than one-eighth Negro blood. Its major features included the following: from a judge. The first code was civil rights, blacks were now able to own land, sell the fruits of their labor and establish their own farm. Under this code also, marriage between blacks was accepted, but it excluded the marriage or any form of relationship between a white and black person. Even though blacks received some freedom under this law, there were still restrictions that differed from them.

Labor Contracts

The South Carolina code included a contract form for black "servants" who agreed to work for white "masters. Under the labor contracts, all business affairs between blacks and whites had to be approved by a judge. . Black servants had to reside on the employer's property, remain quiet and orderly, work from sunup to sunset except on Sundays, and not leave the premises or receive visitors without the master's permission. Masters could "moderately" whip servants under 18 to discipline them. Servants who forfeited their contracts, could be forced to work for less wages

The third code was vagrancy. This code racist content, and still utilized tactics from slavery. The code provided that vagrants could be arrested and imprisoned at hard labor. But the county sheriff could "hire out" black vagrants to a white employer to work off their punishment. Punishment could also consist of the county sheriff offering services or hiring blacks.

Apprenticeship

Southern Black Codes provided another source of labor for white employers—black orphans and the children of vagrants or other destitute parents. Under the codes, South Carolina was able to force black children that were orphaned, to work against their will until 21. Most of the children were kids to parents that were jailed for vagrancy laws. The children could be whipped and punished if they attempted to run away. South Carolina's code replicated the white fixation with governing the previous slaves. It disqualified black individuals from owning most firearms, making or marketing liquor, and coming into the state without first posting a bond for "good behavior." Blacks couldn't sell any product without a written consent from a white employer as the black codes were being implemented, the KKK was on the rise and Jim Crow laws would soon surface. The political racism implemented in the 1800's gave blacks a harsh reality of freedom. Beyond the economic perspective, whites had drawn a deep hatred for blacks, and did not want to identify as equal. This covert racism that existed within the judicial system placed blacks as second-class citizens and were only seen as 3/5 of a man. The racist nature that enslaved Africans, were now making decisions on their freedom. Inequality in wages kept blacks working for past slave owners. The political policies of the 1800's were establishing the future dynamics for years to come. As the southern states created black codes, by the 1900's Jim Crow laws were adopt-ed by 80% of the states. Blacks were free but fell upon hard times, and barely made enough to take care of their families. Next political policies open doors to immigration. Waves of European immigrants flourished into the United States, "Between 1880 and 1920, a time of rapid industrialization and urbanization, America received more than 20 million immigrants. Beginning in the 1890s, the majority of arrivals were from Central, Eastern and Southern Europe. In that decade alone, some 600,000 Italians migrated to America, and by 1920 more than 4 million had entered the United States. Jews from Eastern Europe fleeing religious persecution also arrived in large numbers; over 2 million entered the United States between 1880 and 1920. The peak year for admission of new immigrants was 1907, when approximately 1.3 million people entered the country legally."

Systematically, as slavery ended laws increased, prisons were built, and European immigrant migrated to the country. The Jim Crow laws which were designed for separation, inequality, and injustice however, the only migrants this was subjected to was the African American. European immigrants came to the Americas during the industrial boom, which was a very good time in America. They were welcomed with open arms, and received jobs which paid higher wages than blacks. Immigrants began to get the skill position while blacks remained laborers. The Italian, and Polish built their wealth off illegal activities that went undermined by the government for years. As the European immigrants were getting a warm welcome, black was subjected to white mobs, KKK, police officers, and lynching. These were the physical and psychological combination of racism. These 4 subjects keep the inferiority that was established through slavery alive. Systematically this worked to perfection. The physical elements that were present now, only formulated the PTSD that developed from slavery. Blacks were physically free but still psychologically enslaved, systematically by the KKK freely able to kill and murder blacks, along with low wages, and long hours of work, this was systematically implemented to keep the psychological component of slavery present. The people that made up the black community was comprised of free slaves. White America never allowed blacks to regain their self-esteem, instead they created cartoons, books, plays, and music that degraded black in a humoristic manner, unfortunately the laughter was a pure reality, and the migrants were being socially brainwashed through media, and eventually took the same position as white Americans. Police forces flourished after 1880, the first established police force was in Boston, 1838. Before that, police forces consist of watchmen, and slave catchers.

As slavery ended, these institutions were politically aligned to keep Jim crow laws intact and enforce Laws. Even though during that time, there were union strikes led by Italian, and other immigrant groups. These strikes would get violent, but that would be the only time the police would be policing their own, on the flip side they were enforcing Jim

Crow laws and pumping KKK propaganda. The racist element was re-established through

multiple institutes. The judicial system consists of KKK members, undercover confederate

members which have never died, and has always been present. In the process of all this,

the education system was getting its fair share of racist policies. The discrimination of

blacks during a time when European immigrants were flourishing was now establishing the

social element of blacks for the world to see. Immigrants took a stance against blacks and

eventually took the understanding of white America. During this time social stratification,

and poverty lines were being designed to fit white America. Black would fall right into this

social system because upon leaving slavery, they left with nothing, and as Jim Crow laws

kept them from obtaining equal pay, immigrant was receiving more pay then them. James

Calvin Hemphill, "John Schreiner Reynolds", Men of Mark in South Carolina: Ideals of

American Life Vol. II; Washington, D.C.: Men of Mark Publishing Co., 1908.

Kermit L. Hall, "Political Power and Constitutional Legitimacy: The South Carolina Ku

Klux Klan Trials" Archived 2013-03-16 at the Wayback Machine; Emory Law Journal 33,

Fall 1984.

D. Alan Heslop:Political system/Encyclopædia Britannica March 17, 2017 URL:https://

www.britannica.com/topic/political-system/The-functions-of-government

Burlingame, Michael. "Abraham Lincoln: Domestic Affairs". Charlottesville, Virginia:

Miller Center of Public Affairs, University of Virginia. Retrieved April 14, 2018.

Whittington, Keith E. (March 2000). "Bill Clinton Was No Andrew Johnson: Comparing

Two Impeachments" (PDF). Journal of Constitutional Law. Phila-delphia, Pennsylvania:

University of Pennsylvania. 2 (2): 422–465. Retrieved April 14, 2018

People from different places come to America

They have different backgrounds and have different skin

But they are in America

They should be accepted, even if their from Berlin

And yet we make fun of how they look

And call them names by their background

Because it's a little harder for them to read a book

And we look down on them and frown

Racism is a weird thing

Sometimes we don't even know what it is

Like Mr. KingAnd that dream of his

We shouldn't judge peopleAt any cost

Because their still people Just a little lost

So the next time you see someone

Being made fun of because of their color or background

Don't keep walking and look down

Help and try to fix what has just been done

People are peopleAnd they have feelings tooPeople are people

Just like you Racism Is Not A Crime, But It Should Be

Keegan Shelton

Chapter 4

Birth of a Nation

Power in defense of freedom is greater than power in behalf of tyranny and oppression, because power, real power, comes from our conviction which produces action, uncompromising action.

Malcolm X

The 1800's is the time most should be aware of. This era marked the birth of a nation, the establishment of white infrastructure, and the creation of white privilege. Within the 1800's, slave revolts were uprising all over the country. Slavery had been in play for 200 years, and revolt were becoming the norm, and the white infrastructure felt this would soon become problem. The political climate began to change, and the psychological component of slavery would be implemented. Slavery remains a "contemporary ghost" that shapes African Americans' self-image, their relationships to one another and their relationships with white Americans. (The psychological residuals of slavery 2006). The rebellion's that were uprising were establishing fear in white America. While fear was being established, black were becoming fearless, and choosing to die, versus suffering enslavement for years. The political establishment of the 1800's would inaugurate the Democratic Party and their racist implementation of psychological slavery. The presidents currently were very influential in the future birth of black codes, KKK, and Jim Crow laws. The policy was designed to uplift white civilization, and place whites as a majority, and blacks as a minority. Within the U.S., slaves outnumbered whites, and with rebellion rising, this would be a problem moving forward. Notable presidents responsible for racist political policies, and laws where; James Monroe, Andrew Jackson, Andrew Johnson, Woodrow Wilson, and James Polk. Between 1820-1920, these presidents implemented the racist social structures, institutional racism, and economic racism. Each was driven for white privilege and wealth for years to come. They undermined blacks and looked at them as nothing but economic property to build the wealth of America through cheap labor. Most of the democrats had a tie with the confederate, for most were born in the south. Andrew Johnson, was born in Tennessee and helped the confederate establish black codes. Johnson implemented his own form of Presidential Reconstruction – a series of proclamations directing the seceded states to hold conventions and elections to reform their civil governments. When Southern states returned many of their old leaders and passed Black Codes to deprive the freedmen of many civil liberties. Congressional Republicans refused to seat legislators from those states and advanced legislation to overrule the Southern actions. Johnson vetoed their bills, and Congressional Republicans overrode him, setting a pattern for the remainder of his presidency. Johnson opposed the Fourteenth Amendment, which gave citizenship to former slaves. (Castel, Albert E. (1979).

Andrew Jackson was a wealthy Tennessee enslaver, and responsible for the 1830 Indian removal act. (The Indian Removal Act was signed into law by President Andrew Jackson on May 28, 1830, authorizing the president to grant unsettled lands west of the Mississippi in exchange for Indian lands within existing state borders. A few tribes went peacefully, but many resisted the relocation policy. During the fall and winter of 1838 and 1839, the Cherokees were forcibly moved west by the United States government. Approximately 4,000 Cherokees died on this forced march, which became known as the "Trail of Tears.) (Motes, K.(2017)

James Monroe was born in Virginia; he was the pioneer and initiator of the formation of the American Colonization Society. Woodrow Wilson was also from Virginia; he glorified the Klan and felt as though they were doing a good deed. James Polk was also born in the south, by way of North Carolina. Born is the south does not directly make a person racist, unfortunately looking at the policies and ideologies of each of these presidents, and their influence on political racism, it's clear that their thoughts and perception was the product of a lineage of racist, therefore the barbaric mentality was a taught behavior, and therefore they felt compelled to destruct black civilization. Slavery from a physical sense was now being challenged; the psychological would soon take the place. The 19th century introduced racist concepts that degraded blacks, through psychology, and anthropology. Through these studies, psychologists and anthropologists set out to define the scientific element of race. This process was designed to create a scientific foundation to prove that blacks were inferior, and that white was the original race. These studies searched to prove racial characteristics, mental abilities, and personality traits. (R. Guthrie1998). Psychology was introduced by Wilhelm Wundt, German psychologist who opened the Institute for Experimental Psychology at the University of Leipzig in Germany in 1879. This was the first laboratory dedicated to psychology, and its opening is usually thought of as the beginning of modern psychology. Indeed, Wundt is often regarded as the father of psychology. (Saul Mcleod 2008). The racist biasness and scientific identification of race were founded by Charles Darwin and the concept of social Darwinism through his theory on natural selection. Theories of social selection attempt to explain the success of certain social groups. Based on the laissez faire doctrine, which is racial bias, it interprets the 'survival of the fittest' concept to mean that only the best adapted (those already well off) survive the 'natural conflict' between social groups and thereby enhance the survival capacity of the remaining society. Popular in the 19th and 20th century, this was embraced by Europe and USA Nazis. Darwin's concept on race was defined through his theory of natural selection, and survival of the fittest. Darwin theory on race placed whites on the higher social level, and blacks on the lower. Darwin attempted this theory through different measures. His theory brought on other theories that shaped the consciousness of white and black America. Two of the most recognized were Eugenics, and the Nazi's. One must take note of the importance of what is present at this time. America was taking a different shape for the years to come. The political, and psychological process of the 1800's was socially constructing the world for the future. The psychological thought process that created the social systems was social Darwinism. His theory was practiced by countries that governed the thoughts of the world. "He was committed to a monogenic, rather than the prevailing polygenic, view of human origins, but he still divided humanity into distinct races according to differences in skin, eye or hair color. He was also convinced that evolution was progressive, and that the white races—especially the Europeans—were evolutionarily more advanced than the black races, thus establishing race differences and a racial hierarchy. Darwin's views on gender, too, were utterly conventional."(EMBO Rep. 2009 Apr; 10(4): 297–298)

Darwinism is set to challenge religion and the concept of "all men are created equal." This concept that was stated in the bible was causing the Christian world; especially whites Christian were to challenge slavery. Multiple religious groups were protesting slavery as immoral and condemned in the name of God. Darwinism challenged the bible to only establish white's place in the origin of humanity. The 1800's changed the dynamic for America, escalated racism, and emasculated blacks through psychological theories, and a socially constructed environment. These theories began to invade academia. White students were taught racist ideologies and theories about blacks. As the political system was being run by racist whites, the thought process of whites was being influenced by western psychologists, who received their education in psychology in Germany. Wilhelm Wundt was considered the father of psychology. "Wilhelm Wundt opened the Institute for Experimental Psychology at the University of Leipzig in Germany in 1879. This was the first laboratory dedicated to psychology, and its opening is usually thought of as the beginning of modern psychology. Indeed, Wundt is often regarded as the father of psychology."(McLeod, S. A. (2008). Another figure to be familiar with is Sir Francis Galton. Immediately after the emancipation of the slaves, Galton proposed a new theory into understanding genetic called Eugenics. Galton was the cousin of Charles Darwin.(W. Nobles1986). "in 1869 Galton published his work on hereditary genius and stated that on the average intellectual scale, negroes were at least 2 grades lower than whites. (W.Nobles 1986). Galton was motivated to promote the idea of racial improvement through selective mating and sterilizing of the unfit. (cf.Galton 1869) Galton believed that blacks were the lower race to whites, and to rid the world of all the unfit, they must sterilize the unfit. Nazis had utilized Galton, and Darwin theory to implement their own extermination. Germans were responsible for not only trying to exterminate the Jews; they were responsible for slaughtering between 1,000 and 10,000 Africans. "The worldwide Eugenics movement gained strength in the U.S. at the end of the 1890s, when theories of selective breeding espoused by British anthropologist Francis Galton and his prototypes Karl Pearson, gained currency. Connecticut was the first of many states, beginning in 1896, to pass marriage laws with eugenic provisions, prohibiting anyone who was "epileptic, imbecile or feeble-minded" from marrying. The noted American biologist, Charles Davenport, became the director of biological research at a station in Cold Spring Harbor in New York in 1898. Six years later the Carnegie Institute provided the funding for Davenport to create the Station for Experimental Evolution. Then, in 1910, Davenport and Harry H. Laughlin took advantage of their positions at the Eugenics Record Office to promote eugenics." Considering the things that socially construct the environment to affect blacks, white America utilized every angle to keep blacks from rising. The Eugenics movement was established off principles of Charles Darwin's natural selection and survival of the fittest. A major influence on the eugenics movement was Herbert Spencer, an English philosopher and prominent political theorist. Spencer is best known as the father of social Darwinism, a school of thought that applied the evolutionary theory of "survival of the fittest"—a phrase coined by Spencer—to human societies.

The political system implemented structures to keep blacks from rising, the psychological thought that was being defined by western psychologists was invading the academic books, and teaching the white population false ideologies about blacks, therefore constructing their thinking to a bias, and racist outlook when it came to blacks. The first weapon was religion, a statement that whites utilized to justify the wrongdoing was becoming accepted by the population. The misuse of bible scriptures was the first stage of emasculating blacks. By the 1800, laws were established based on biased perspectives that were falsely justified by scriptures in the bible. As the economy began to grow in the 1800's the political climate took the approach of keep the economic enslavement relevant while preaching freedom to slaves. The civil war was the first stage of hope for black America. Entertainment was making it's way into the Americas, and black minstrels would keep the degradation of blacks prevalent from a comical stand point. As the civil war ended, Lincoln, emancipated the slaves, but his life would get cut down 3 days later. By December of that year, the states ratified the 13th amendment.

13th Amendment Amendment XIII

Section 1.

Neither slavery nor involuntary servitude, except as a punishment for crime whereof the party shall have been duly convicted, shall exist within the United States, or any place subject to their jurisdiction.

Chapter 5

The Birth of White Privilege

The appeal to the white man's pocket has ever been more effective than all the appeals ever made to his conscience.

Ida B. Wells

The academia created the bias, and prejudice nature of society, which were formulated from racist political policies. Historians, naturalists, anthropologists, psychologists and other racist members of the white community led the academia. Books were published, articles were written, and false scientific theories about blacks were published for public knowledge, and part of the school's curriculum. This was a learned behavior that was embedded in the mindset of white America at present. The academia not only degraded blacks, but the textbooks were also defining whites as superior to blacks, and the commonality with apelike characteristics. Science published books, were utilized in Germany and USA they were used thoroughly. Count Arthur de Gobineau, in a 1854 book stated "the white, yellow, and black race are unequal and that the 'Aryans' were not only superior to all other races."(bergman2004). Many coined the Darwin term and placed their own perspective. Darwin opposed slavery, and most of his studies and research was based off plants, and animals. Gobineau believed that Aryans, which he classified as the dominant race, from intermarried with members of a lower race, this is causing the decline of the dominant race. George Hunter titled a book, called Civic Biology '' which was the most widely used life science textbooks. In a chapter, the races of man, broke the population down in five races, ranking lowest to highest, the lowest was the Ethiopian or negro type, originated in Africa. Next was the Malay, or brown race, the American Indian, China, Japan, and the Eskimo's, and the highest level was white, the Caucasian, civilized white inhabitant of Europe. "Negligence, slowness, cunning, and phlegmatic, In 1853, Bremeister published his book, the" black man" Stated, "it is not worthwhile to look into the soul of the negro, it is the judgment of god, which is being executed, at the approach of civilization, the savage man must perish. (Brewmeister 1853).

Sir Frances Galton, who founded the eugenics movement proposed a science of heredity,

He believed that blacks were grossly inferior to whites, even the lowest grade of white.

(W.Nobles1986) Galton stood on the sterilization of the unfit, which he considered

was the present-day negro. As European's implemented the racial scales, the western

world embraced it and began using it to psychologically enslave the mindset of blacks.

Herbert Spencer, an English philosopher, who influenced the psychological thinking in

America, believed that the suffering of the poor was nature's mechanism for ensuring

the survival of the fittest.(1896 principles of psychology). In 1916, Ferguson theorized

that black people were intelligent in proportion to the white blood they posed. (W.Nobles

1986). There were an abundance of scholars, professors, and psychologists that used a

biased, and racist perspective when falsely scientifically defining the origin of race. This

information flooded the library, and the intellectual dialogue's by so-called scholars.

The feeble-minded uneducated whites took bits and pieces to define their stance of

racism in a justified manner. Inferior races," eugenic theorists concluded, were a drain

on the economic, political and moral health of American life. Some African American

intellectuals, too, supported the theory, arguing we should focus on the "talented tenth"

of every race." This statement dealt a crippling blow, as blacks began to enter academia,

some began to accept this perspective, and actually teach it. German Nazi's took the

Eugenics theory to the extreme, not only did they slaughter over six million Jews, they

slaughter 1000's of Africans." Shark Island Concentration Camp or "Death Island"

was a concentration camp on Shark Island off Luderitz, Namibia. It was used by the

German empire during the Herero and Namaqua Genocide of 1904-1908. During this

time between 1,032 and 3000 Herero and Namaqua men, women, and children died

in the camp. The Hereo is an ethnic group inhabiting parts of Southern Africa. The

concentration camps consisted of people who were skin-and-bone, mass graves, and

medical experiments.

CRIME & REASON: A BLACK CHOICE

Eugenics and the birth of discriminatory prejudices

Eugenics, the set of beliefs and practices which aims at improving the genetic quality of the
human population, played a significant role in the history and culture of the United States
prior to its involvement in World War II.

Eugenics offered Americans in positions of power an authoritative scientific language to
substantiate their biases against those they feared as dangerous. America has been adopting
the concept from Germany since the 1800's and have been allies since this time. A strategic
ploy by white politicians took place in, "between 1830-1860, (take in consideration Andrew
Jackson was elected president 1829) New York grew from 197,000 to 806,000 residents.
At the same time, Philadelphia's population grew from 80,000 to 566,000 and Boston's
population increased from 61,000 to 178,000. The first wave of immigrants between 1820
and 1860 bought 5 million new immigrants to America, and the second wave between
1860-1890 brought an additional 13.5 million. In New York 3.5 million immigrants arrived
between 1820-1860, and by 1855 half of the population was foreign-born German and
Irish." (Kuntz1988) This increase in population was set to contribute to the white race for
the said theoretical approach to increase the white population in numbers to surpass blacks,
and natives. This was done strategically as the economy was booming in the northern
areas, instead of allowing blacks the first opportunity at industrial work; jobs were being
occupied by German and Irish immigrants. The key perspective of this theory is looking
at the census, from 1820. Each year from 1860 to present, the census broke down all other
groups, placing them in their own categories. The only groups of immigrants that weren't
forced to identify separately were the European immigrants, they had to identify as white.
This was intentionally done to increase white population and place everyone else at a
minority. As the population within America increased, so did the social hierarchy. This
influx of Europeans seemed as if it was strategically done to keep blacks from obtaining
any wealth from the new industrial boom. By allowing a large number of Europeans to
migrate, this made it harder for blacks to get ahead. Blacks in 1890, had to identify as

26

black, Mulatto, Quadroon, or octoroon as the industrial economy boomed, America had recently completed the initial phase of of establishing mental slavery. Looking at the census report, whites, no matter immigrant, or civilian, they only identified as white, not German American, nor Irish-American. Industrialization. "German Americans are the largest of the ancestry groups reported by the US Census Bureau in its American Community Survey." The industrial revolution in Germany pushed many to migrate to the American Midwest, where they could continue to work as independent craftsmen or farmers. In Wisconsin, Peter Glass farmed and used his woodworking skills while embracing his adopted country. He became an American citizen and made furniture that incorporated U.S. patriotic and historical motifs.

Germans were the largest foreign language group at the time. The majority moved to the Midwestern "German triangle," between Missouri, Ohio, and Wisconsin. Many were farmers in their homeland and pursued the same livelihood in the Midwest. Living in close proximity to other Germans encouraged these immigrants to maintain traditional customs and language. The anti-immigration sentiment so prevalent in some U.S. cities gained less ground in the rural areas of the Midwest. By the second generation, most European families that came over in poverty were already experiencing family wealth, and by the 3rd generation, the family wealth was established through all of the work provided through the industrial boom that placed America at an economic power. "Eugenics". Unified Medical Language System (Psychological Index Terms). National Library of Medicine. 26 September 2010.

Chapter 6

Introduction into Black Consciousness.

I believe in Liberty for all men: the space to stretch their arms and their souls, the right to breathe and the right to vote, the freedom to choose their friends, enjoy the sunshine, and ride on the railroads, uncursed by color; thinking, dreaming, working as they will in a kingdom of beauty and love.

W. E. B. Du Bois

Defining black consciousness understands the ideology of what it is to be black in the United states.. Understanding of the term is first identifying the thought. What is the thought when one defines themselves as black? Is it a rebellion from the term African American, or is it just an expression of defining one through color? What tone is used when one states', "I'm black." Is it the first stage of consciousness, and a disassociation from African American? Is there emotional expression when one calls themselves black? It's used to combat racism? Let's look at the way black is commonly used in one's expression. "Well, being that we are black we have one strike against." "That only happened to him because he was black." "They don't care, they're only black in their eyes." These are some of the negative ways black is expressed. There is an abundance of positivity, black has always expressed a distinctive beauty from the rest. The purpose I'm attempting to define is why has African American become comfortable with identifying as black instead. What does African American mean to the person that identifies as black. Or what has affected the visual perception that has shifted the identity. Is stating that you're black, disassociating with African and American people? What effect of the term, African American, does it truly expound upon? Have blacks systematically dropped the term African American?

The war within: conscious revolution

The war within, is a theoretical approach used to define the term double consciousness. Dual consciousness looks at two thoughts that conflict to cause social and psychological issues. Is defining as black, a state of freedom? And if so, what would make African

American the counter of freedom, which would be enslavement? Could identifying as African American possess a dual consciousness re-identifying with two cultural perspectives that conflict in history? The cultural perspective of conflict is the identification with being African, and American. From a theoretical view, this is part of the psychological enslavement, and these dual perspectives are always at war, combating the other for dominance. These dual perspectives are; African and American. The American history of blacks entails a gruesome history that contributes to genetic disposition within blacks. I will use a simple analogy to get the reader to understand the point I am attempting to make.

Analogy of African and AmericanTake a child, adopted at the age of one, growing within a family that consists of three siblings, and a two-parent home. Prominent home, 10 years later at the age of 11, the crucial blow of coming to grips with the mere fact that your siblings are not your siblings, and your parents are not your parents. Place yourself in those shoes; the mind wonders and thoughts formulate that grant understanding to questions of the past. You see clearer into the facts now, behavior's may even popup that one didn't understand, but now make sense. The person placed in this situation will go through a psychological change, and even though this has been his home since birth, he now feels unwelcome. Depression, and stress anxiety sets in, his mood changes, as well as his behavior in school. This is symbolic of being black in America. To feel unwanted in a country that you have been in your whole life, and even though your life has been good, the identification with your race and America makes you always feel detached from being American. The same psychological changes that the boy is experiencing, can be figments of his imagination, but knowing that he is not looked at as American in the eyes of America, (symbolic to his adopted family) the feeling is like being on an island with everything you need, but knowing this is not where you belong.

The opposite, looking at the identification into being African from the same example. The boy now finds out that he is not looked at as a true American in the eyes of his sibling.

He now searches out for his birth parents; he is elated at the fact that he can find out who his birth parents are. He searches and eventually finds out his birth name is Africa. He searches and seeks to make contact through social services, only to find out that Africa does not want to accept him. From that the boy is now distraught; he can't say he is an American, because his sibling seems distant with his newfound knowledge of self. He reflects on all the time he felt favoritism, and when he received clothes and sneakers of a lesser amount then his siblings. He says to himself, all the long, they knew, and I was blind to the fact, when the facts were clear in their behavior. His second thought kicks in. I can't even say I'm African, they don't wasn't anything to do with me, and I am in this position because of them, his mind became angered at the fact that here he was giving into adoption, and now that he has discovered the truth, his own people do not want anything to do with him. The biggest issue here is cultural identification. Cultural identification is important for a person's progression through life. Identification with an attachment gives a sense of pride. The African American doesn't possess pride; he or she doesn't feel the attachment to being African, nor American. This double consciousness is the warring consciousness that blacks in America must decipher through. In the process, other social factor contributes to black's self-esteem, constant discrimination, prejudice, racism, and injustice.

Chapter 7

Part 1: The Emergence of the New Negro

No universal selfishness can bring social good to all. Communism - the effort to give all men what they need and to ask of each the best they can contribute - this is the only way of human life.

W. E. B. Du Bois

For the Negro, Andrew Johnson did less than nothing when once he realized that the chief beneficiary of labor and economic reform in the South would be freedmen. His inability to picture Negroes as men made him oppose efforts to give them land; oppose national efforts to educate them; and above all things, oppose their rights to vote.. (Du Bois n.d.)

The new Negro was defining as a new form of black consciousness that emerged from the reconstruction era. Within this era birthed a prolific influential group of African American that would leave a legacy behind. Among this group were scholars, educators, actors, and activists who fought to reconstruct African Americans. One of the most re-known members of this group was W.E.B. Du Bois. He was an American sociologist, historian, civil rights activist, and active member of Garvey's Pan African movement. Credible to his name, Du Bois has written over a 100 books, letters, poems, and newspaper articles. His literature can be identified as a course work toward the understanding of being black in America.

Du Bois was a prolific author. Within his collection of essays, he expressed a deep passion in transforming the African American race. The Souls of Black folk was a seminal work in African-American literature; and his 1935 Black Reconstruction in America challenged the prevailing orthodoxy that blacks were responsible for the failures of the Reconstruction Era. Within the text, one will evaluate W.E.B. Dubois literature, his concept of double consciousness along with classical essays, the soul of black folks, black reconstruction in America, and his famous debate with Booker t Washington.

W.E.B. Dubois coined the term double consciousness in 1903 "the negro is a sort of seventh son, born with a veil, and gifted with second sight in this American world—a world which yields him no true self-consciousness, but only lets him see himself through the revelation of the other world. One ever feels his twoness—an American, a negro; two souls, two thoughts, two unreconciled strivings; two warring ideals in one dark body, whose dogged strength alone keeps it from being torn asunder (Dubois,1965, p.215

Double consciousness defines the mental representation to understand the concept behind the way blacks process and identify with information. Dubois expresses how being black in America you are conformed to interpret your identity into two different consciousness, furthermore, negating the development of the true self-consciousness which places a deep level of insecurity, and self-esteem issue on the said person. What is to be black and American? To be black, to be brown, to born under the guise as one of god's greatest creation to civilization, yet and still we claw at our skin in a quest for why my pigmentation brings racism, injustice, discrimination, lack of equality, and the worst of the worst condition, yet I seek refuge with my own flesh, which is identical to the sun that god created, my pigmentation, and melamine is my stamp of approval!! Yet, and still, I possess this understanding with confusion, is this what it is to be black, or brown. I too am America, they say, what is American, what is the land of the free, the land of freedom, justice, and equality that is spoken in the national anthem, and star spangled banner. Have blacks identified with those privileges? Or shall we say that black America identify with privilege through discrimination, poverty, and low socio-economic status. Or should I say have blacks been treated equally in freedom, justice, and equality. The answer is evident, unfortunately these are the issues at the central point of double consciousness. Being black and American you are forced to see yourself through the eyes of the oppressor with the intention of seeking approval. Being black you're forced to see your image tarnished over the news and media before you can identify with who you are as a person. Then living within a society where your identified as being African American, where natives of the African continent tend to look down on you due to how society has projected you. Secondly, you can't see yourself as American because you don't receive equal treatment as fellow Americans. Classified as being African American leaves one with a double consciousness, which consists of not being able to 100% percent attach to either due to lack of full acceptance. This inconsistency causes one to lack identification with their true self, which results in insecurities, esteem issues, and deferred dreams. Social environment becomes affected with the results of double consciousness causing social dilemma's leading to negative results. These negative results along with social injustice, and discrimination led too black on black crime, poverty and psychological problems by way of social development due to double consciousness. By possessing two thoughts, one can never come to grips with self-identity. Lack of self-identity, inconsistency of character, and worst of all social conformity affects the developmental stages for blacks. Understanding Dubois's double consciousness from a social and psychological perspective opens up a portal of understanding into the depth of the black situation. Written in 1903, the soul of black folks gave a vivid interpretation into understanding the consciousness of the Negro. 113 years to the present year, double consciousness is still prevalent within blacks, unfortunately the effect has doubled, with others factors becoming present that weren't present during Dubois time. At the present date, blacks have more to factor into their consciousness than they did in 1903. That reason being, in 1903, black had less advantages and Jim Crow was in full swing. In 1903 in comparison to 2021, black was segregated and denied rights as human being; morally, and religiously, education was scarce and sad to say, it was the norm to accept racism, hate, discrimination, inequality, and injustice by way of white supremacy. In 2021, blacks are not segregated, nor denied educational rights, and the opportunity to design their life. Yes, discrimination, racism, injustice, and inequality are still present, however the most important factor is distributed equally, and that the opportunity to obtain an education, and READ!!! Another factor that was not present during Dubois time was the race discrimination amongst the victims of the trans-Atlantic slave trade that is present in 2021. Discrimination consists of hatred, ridicule, and racism amongst Caribbean, African, and African American blacks. Separatism would never be a thought in Dubois eyes, for none of the forefathers of black consciousness ever considered the separatism amongst the victim of the Trans-Atlantic slave trade would be such an effect on the advancement of blacks. During Dubois time, double consciousness only consisted of how you were seen through white eyes as a Negro, and an American, in 2021 your consciousness as a black consists of how you are seen in the eyes of whites, Caribbean's, Latino's, Africans, and your own. Taking this into account; along with injustice and social inequalities, as well as a lack of education, is it possible to develop no conscious, after faced with no self-identity, and discrimination? Can this be the reason for the high rate of black-on-black crime?

Dubois's term double consciousness, looked at from a psychological perspective, gives vivid detail into the social and developmental psychology of blacks and the reason for today's problem. Dubois' term shows pure genius and shows a supreme intellect that addresses the issue of black America.

Chapter 8

Understanding Double Consciousness: Social Dilemma's

It is a peculiar sensation, this double-consciousness, this sense of always looking at one's self through the eyes of others, of measuring one's soul by the tape of a world that looks on in amused contempt and pity. One ever feels his two-ness,—an American, a Negro; two souls, two thoughts, two unreconciled strivings; two warring ideals in one dark body, whose dogged strength alone keeps it from being torn asunder. The history of the American Negro is the history of this strife — this longing to attain self-conscious manhood, to merge his double self into a better and truer self. In this merging he wishes neither of the older selves to be lost. He does not wish to Africanize America, for America has too much to teach the world and Africa. He wouldn't bleach his Negro blood in a flood of white Americanism, for he knows that Negro blood has a message for the world. He simply wishes to make it possible for a man to be both a Negro and an American without being cursed and spit upon by his fellows, without having the doors of opportunity closed roughly in his face.

W.E.B. Du Bois (The Souls of Black Folk)

The Talented Tenth of the Negro race must be made leaders of thought and missionaries of culture among their people. W. E. B. Du Bois

Understanding double consciousness in 2021, displays a different perspective versus Dubois's 1903 version. Blacks possess a double consciousness that consists of 2 thoughts, 2 perspectives, and 2 social views that derive from biological, social, and environmental factors. Two thoughts, consist of searching for one's identity, blacks being identified as African American, have no attachment and stake to being African, nor American. "a shared complexion does not equal a shared culture. Whether we like it or not, Africans and African American have two distinct cultures." Dubois and other would never think that it would be so much conflict amongst the descendants of the trans-Atlantic slave trade. "In any case, the modern world must remember that in this age when the ends of the world are being brought so near together the millions of black men in Africa, America and the islands of the sea, not to speak of the brown and yellow myriads elsewhere, are bound to have great influence upon the world in the future." W.E.B DuBois, to the nations of the world july1900). From looking at Dubois words, title to the nations of the world, his words depict freedom and unity amongst all the African descendants with the ideology as this being a cause that will in the future have greater influence upon the world. This greater influence that Dubois speaks of, is blacks having a greater say in political and economic issues that financially can establish a foundation to build upon. With the unity of all African descendants for a greater cause, this would restore the balance within the justice and economic system, giving the darker race a better place in the world. Unfortunately, at present, which is a mere figment of the past that has become so detrimental that restoring a connection is almost astronomical. This friction causes turmoil between the two leaving no room for unity, nor for black to attach to their African ancestry. Blacks neither can attach to being identified with being American due to our history within America, has not been a pleasant one. Psychologically, this affects the total population, by not identifying with a culture of their own, this causes personality issues, and inferiority. The psychological effect of not possessing an attachment to a true identification, causes media and social influence, this may explain why so many conform to gangs. With nothing to consider their own, gangs may band together to establish their own foundation instead of conforming to someone else's. Next, we have two perspectives, inferiority, and conformity. African Americans are victims of inferiority, this is due to lack of self-identification, which results from conforming to groups, organizations, and religious beliefs that have no solid foundation for blacks to identify as their own. Inferiority is a major issue within black Americans, the dynamic leads to insecurities, and confidence issues when it comes to dealing with whites. Last, we have two social views, which is seen through social inequality, and social injustice. injustice and inequality within black communities assist in establishing social views for blacks, with discrimination, racism, and prejudice being central point of black's social views. The reason the social views are seen through this view, is within black communities, blacks identify with injustice within the legal system at an all-time high, and deal with inequality with the social world. When identifying with the social world, we must investigate social psychology. Social psychology is a study that focuses on the attributes such as thoughts, behaviors, and feelings which are influenced by the real or imaginative presence of others. From a sociological view, social issues, and stress that are prevalent within a community will eventually become part of the chain of social factors. Society has given the black race a negative disposition within the world. The negative behavior that has been associated with blacks has become the automatic thinking to a large percentage of nonblack Americans. An Implicit Association Test (I.A.T.), which is a test to measure unconscious prejudices according to speed with which people can pair a target face with a positive or negative association. (Banaji & Greenwald, 2013). Within Implicit prejudices, most do not identify with being prejudiced until put to the test. One test study showed that people responded faster when white faces were shown with a positive situation, then black faces with a positive situation. Even in some cases blacks responded slower to positive attributes toward blacks than whites did. Implicit prejudices are associated with a person's automatic thinking, this automatic thinking derives from implicit prejudices, and racial discrimination. Factoring in all the above, the consciousness of blacks is distorted, and unsecure. As Dubois stated, "two souls, two thoughts, two unreconciled strivings: two warring ideals in one dark body. "From being viewed from so many eyes in a negative sense, but looking at yourself and knowing your capabilities but afraid to display due to inferiority, will play within the psyche of anyone. Social psychology studies have displayed many racial and discriminatory factor that effect the growth and development of blacks. Larger part of the world is prone to look at blacks from a negative perspective before accepting their positives. These behaviors are displayed by non-black Africans and affect blacks to the point where they began to live to impress others in position then their own self. This is common within the work world. The above are issues that distinguish directly

CRIME & REASON: A BLACK CHOICE

from a double consciousness. If black had their own self-consciousness, their concerns would not be based on public views. Unfortunately, with wealth and success associated with being white, the understanding is clear why some conform to inferiority by way of capitalism. especially with blacks that are from poverty-stricken area, and suburban areas also. Results of the above, leads me to believe that most that lack attachment to an identity, will eventually become persuaded through media depiction. Looking within the community of black Americans, most follow trends of rappers, actors, and actresses. Media depiction plays heavily into the consciousness of blacks, they began to spend money obtaining material things to appear on the surface as if their life is great, when all actuality it is pulling them further and further away from the truth.

Chapter 9

The Importance of Self-Consciousness

The history of the American Negro is the history of this strife,—this longing to attain self-conscious manhood, to merge his double self into a better and truer self

W.E.B. Du Bois (The Souls of Black Folk)

"The living conditions for black began deteriorating, and with the sure knowledge that we are slated for destruction, we have been transformed into an implacable army of liberation." (George Jackson 1971) self-consciousness is an acute sense of self awareness, preoccupied with self, and having a confident personality. Self-consciousness has different levels that affect behaviors in various ways. One view is through a psychological view, which is private and public self-consciousness. Who we are in private is masked by the character we display in public? The importance of self-consciousness is more important to the development of a group than any other variable. Lack of self-consciousness leaves one contemplating with doubt when crucial judgment is involved. Most people or might I say from statistical reports, most leaders have high self-consciousness, and confidence. Lack of, has multiple variables that affect the population, which influences the cognition, making self-consciousness an important factor in the development of a social group. Meaning, if most of a group's thoughts are processed through lack of self-consciousness, that vast majority's ways of processes will affect the total population. This lack of, in my perspective, is due to double consciousness which is thoughts processed and social conditioning accepted because one has no true origin to develop a sense of pride with. Example, all nationalities and ethnic groups have a flag they can call their own that has an attachment and stake to their ancestry and roots. Dominican, Haitian, Jamaican, African, and all origins that distinguish from Africa have their own culture and moral value to attach to. They have their parades, and they go back to their country sometimes 2 to 3 times a year. Us, as blacks in America, honestly out of the 47 countries in Africa, we cannot decipher which country our ancestry derived from to even attach to a designated origin.

CRIME & REASON: A BLACK CHOICE

Our parades consist of African day parades, unfortunately these parades are consumed by more black Americans, than birthright Africans. I speak about this because having a flag or country you can go back to and revisit your past, is crucial to the development of self-identification. When you can proudly and boastfully say, I'm Jamaican, or any of the above, it creates a will power to succeed. It's not a coincidence that most that come over from other countries obtain success, they have an attachment to a greater cause, and that helps their people survive. This explains my theory on, once the social cognition of a group becomes the social norm by the vast majority, the outcome will develop the social conditioning, which in return helps establish identity. Once this becomes the social norm, and the behaviors are repeated, it now becomes the psychological process of thinking of the said ethnic group. I make reference to the psychological view so we maintain direction and visual perspective of Dubois's double consciousness." two souls, two thoughts, two unreconciled strivings; two warring ideals in one dark body," the psychological view represents the above statement, as black Americans, in public we display a maladaptive, inferior, and insubordinate feature when it comes to dealing with the rest of the world, due to the fact, by not possess an identity, some chose to make it their business to quote on quote fit in with the IN!! However, in private, we display denial to our psychological conditioning that we chose to display to the masses, but when it comes to our own, we are aggressive, jealous, hateful, envious and seek to destroy each other at all cost. For example, a Blackman or black woman can gain notoriety for their intellect and their passion for pursuing the rights and justice for blacks, just as that said person began to gain media exposure, you will see so called intellectual blacks that have done nothing for the people as a whole use derogatory and defamation of character when discuss the persons that is receiving media attention. Just look at how once DR Umar Johnson was caught up in an allegation, you watched his own people destroy and patronize his character, even though some points made were accurate, however the behavior is the focus. One should ask themselves, why. Why after understanding the plight that African descendants went to get

40

where they are now, why is it that their own are at the finger of the trigger aimed to destroy one's ideology, views, and instruction for the betterment of the race. Is it that some began to hate their conditions so much that they begin to become racist toward their own because it's a mirror image of themselves that is covered under layers of denial and self-hate that's not identified with due to lack of self-consciousness?

Consciousness can be viewed as high self-conscious, and low self-conscious, the two differ and affect the psychological views of a person differently depending on social and environmental factors. These factors have varying degrees of measurements. People with a high self-consciousness are more aware and confident within their personality and appearance. They know themselves objectively, while people with a low self-consciousness are associated with shyness and embarrassment which more than likely the person will display a low sense of pride. Low self-conscious people are more concerned with how other people see them, versus how they see themselves. This is the concept that establishes a double consciousness, seeing yourself as how you are viewed, more than how you see yourself. Eventually how others see you will become your characteristic, you will be more prone to what is accepted versus what you enjoy.

Looking at self-consciousness through a social psychology point of view, consciousness The group will shape the social environment based on what is the social norm. How does having a double consciousness affect a social environment? If most of the population possess a double consciousness, that means the social environment will create social stressor based on the psychological process that develops social cognition. The elements mentioned affect an environment more than what is identified on the surface. One example, if a group process is thought identical, the outcome of those thoughts will eventually develop a social perspective which later develops into a social dilemma.

Social environments are determined by what most of the people in the community contribute to the social conditions. If 7 out of 10 homes are single parents with multiple children, the effects of those 7 homes will have a greater influence on the community than the 3 homes with two parents. Within the 3 homes that possess two parents, adequate funds, the children from one of those homes will fall victim to the environment. With lack of understanding into the dynamics of the topic, those 8 homes that succumbed to the environment are 3 to 4 generations into this mindset, still living the same, and in some communities the same places.

The above circumstances are what make the issue more psychological than anything. The reason being, once the social stressors in the environment have developed into the social norm, over a process of time, it becomes psychological. The generations before are victims of circumstance that blacks endured due to double consciousness, but; why are the generation after or at present still victims of the same behaviors. Examples are before them, yet and still we as a People have a high poverty and recidivism rate. Who is the blame for recidivism? Is it the repeat offender, or the judicial system? If the majority consist of single parent homes, domestic abuse, and lack of adequate finances, eventually the condition of the house that develop the social perception and understanding of the social environment, Those issues will soon affect the population in total.

Chapter 10

Developmental Psychology

Usually the black racist has been produced by the white racist. In most cases where you see it, it is the reaction to white racism, and if you analyze it closely, it's not really black racism... If we react to white racism with a violent reaction, to me that's not black racism. If you come to put a rope around my neck and I hang you for it, to me that's not racism. Yours is racism, but my reaction has nothing to do with racism...

Malcolm X

Our nation's oldest sin and deepest crime is the isolation of minority children - black children, in particular - in schools that are not only segregated but shamefully unequal.

Jonathan Kozol

From the first two chapters, the understanding that has been defined has given visual perspective into social psychological situations that contribute to the environmental factors in Black communities. However, the developmental factor is vital to social issues. Developmental psychology analyzes how human beings develop over time. However, this book will give my visual perspective into developmental psychology and how it plays a major part in the shaping of black environments. Developmental psychology helps gain an insight into the developmental stages across the board from an ethical aspect. I say ethical, because culturally the developmental progress is different culturally. Meaning, culturally we are different, so our developmental and social issues differ which makes our progression different through the stages of life. This book is designated to adhere to the black in western culture that shows disturbances during the most prominent developmental stages. Developments start within the household. Family structures are broken down into three, however, our focus will be single parent homes, and nuclear families. Children growing up in either home developmental stage differ. Looking at black within the United States, in comparison to blacks from other continents, family structure is the most crucial element to understand to identify with the issue within the black communities. A high percentage of black suffer from single parent homes. Single parent homes within the black communities place a high volume of pressure on the single parent which mostly consists of a single mother. The dynamics of the black families have declined so much to where the father side of most children has none or little interaction with the child, leaving the mother to fend on her own in some cases with no help at all. A large percentage of single parent homes consist of more than one child, which doubles the mother or father's responsibility. By the woman taking on more responsibility which is to aid in the betterment of her child that means there is less time for nurturing. Lack of nurturing is detrimental to the development of children. Single mothers that are ambitious and career grounded tend to take on more responsibilities such as more work and school to help better the future of the child. The second single parent is the woman that does absolutely nothing. When I say nothing, I am referring to women that utilize the system as a means of survival, and nurturing. Looking at the two types of single parents, we can now focus on the behaviors and thoughts that differ from the two, but also how they affect the social environment and contribute to the social factors that are destroying our communities. Let us look at what I consider the ambitious single parent, her mind works in many ways, and her passion is driven by her current situation and the psychological stress that adds to it places her under high stress. Now let us look at the indolent single parent. Her days consist of lounging around doing nothing for the advancement of herself nor her children. A high percent of the indolent single parents has some form of addictions, ranging from marijuana, crack, cocaine, heroin, and a slew of other drugs that are now relevant within black communities. Another keynote that should be taken into consideration is the psychological effect of domestic violence which would be discussed later in the chapter. Looking at single parents both ambitious and indolent, they both suffer from a high percentage of domestic violence, by way of the children's fathers, or the boyfriend. Some women within black communities go through every relationship with some type of domestic abuse present. As we investigate the dynamics of each home that consist of single parenting, we should now be able to focus on the topic at hand which Is crime and reason: a black choice. Both children will lack the equal balance of nutrients that is required.

In this text I chose to view nature versus nurture as a disposition into the subject. Looking at nature versus nature, a black perspective, I will focus on how this theory can be co-joined with Lev Vygotsky theory, which he focused on the role of cultural influence that will be the determining factor in a child's development which moves from the social level to the individual level. Vygotsky claimed that psychology should focus on the progress of human consciousness through the relationship of an individual and their environment. Vygotsky theory on human consciousness progresses through the relationship an individual has with their environment, I am in total agreement with. his perspective that a child's development moves from social level to the individual level which in turn becomes psychological. The central point of this chapter is developmental psychology within the black community. The developmental stages occur through the age of 0-12 which is where the importance of the household plays into effect. If the adults of the home are victims of the social conditions that plague the inner city, the children will develop the same social ideology as the adults. The development of the child during this age is where the social cognition begins to develop. Social cognition is developed through perception that has become an automatic thinking. Going back into chapter two, where we discussed self-consciousness and DuBois's double consciousness, we can now formulate an understanding into the psycho effect of double consciousness. When a home becomes influenced by social influence, along with lack of education, the children within the home will have a hindrance in their development. Let's analyze a single mother, three children, two different fathers', neither present. The children living within the ambitious single parent will be forced to mature and take on responsibilities that precede them. The older child usually becomes the caretaker of the younger, and the children either spend a lot of time home alone, or at the homes of relatives while the parent is at work. Focusing on what's being discussed brings me to nature vs nature. Children in single parent homes take a natural instinct toward life that reason being, by spending a lot of time alone while the parent is at work, leaves room for the social environment to take an effect on the child. They begin to do what is natural to survive during the time their parents are at work. By the age of 9-12, most children begin to indulge in outside activities. These outside activities are crucial to the development of a child's social cognition especially in the inner city where the streets are crime and drug ridden. Now looking at the indolent single parent, she is home all day but never with her children. The dysfunction of this home produces a high percentage of domestic violence, and conduct disorder begins to display from the child while in school. The homes more than likely consist of drug and alcohol abuse along with domestic violence. Now look at the social influences along with the predicament being discussed. The social influences are drugs, violence, and music. Inner city kids from dysfunctional homes are prone to be influenced by music. Listening to the music, one can interpret the influence that is taking effect on the child that lacks proper nurture and result in its natural habitat as a means of survival, and identification into self-identification. The streets of the inner city, the ones committing the crimes, and killing one another are none other than the children that were subjected to the homes above. The child takes on the approach of the majority and begins to view things socially from the same perspective. One reason is due to the parent not being present during crucial times of nurture. The current most widespread outcome in cases involving single parenting within black communities is delinquent juveniles. The next few pages, we will analyze what the outcome has become in recent years. Observing the dilemma that exists within black communities, I will show information based on correlation study to determine how single parenting has affected our neighborhoods. For future purposes, this issue will need to be addressed, if not we stand to get left behind even more. Information up to date has developed statistics to develop the theory involving the black family, also known as black matriarchy. The term black matriarchy is a term utilized to express black American families that are led by women. 7 out of 10 homes are run by women, either an ambitious single parent or an indolent single parent. Focusing on the effects of single parenting can assist in what is transpiring throughout the developmental stages to give us insight into the social issues that plague inner cities. The issue that needs to be focused upon is the increase in violent black on black crime. Studies involving the breakdown of the black family were performed in 1965, by Daniel Patrick Moynihan, in the Moynihan report. "The current most widespread African American family structure consisting of a single parent has historic roots dating back to 1880. Data from U.S. census reports reveal that between 1880 and 1960, married households consisting of two parents were the most widespread form of African American family structures." (Ruggles, S. 1994) At the brink of the emancipation proclamation, one can see that the most valuable element to move on pass slavery and into the reconstruction era was to maintain the importance of family. No matter the situation, the family still maintained its structure. Maintaining family structure is crucial to the development of a group, for the dynamics The home is what assists into the development of the social conditions that cause social dilemmas and social stress.

These stressors began to invade the environment, and eventually they became the norm after so many years. Generation that falls victim to the vicious cycle of poverty, that is not only a physical component, but the mental components have a high chance of developing criminal behavior.

The mental aspect of poverty, places people with despair and depression.

Poverty places inner city youth at the foot of crime, not because they are criminals, but as a mere means of survival, especially in the indolent single parent care. Most children identify with poverty and the psychological effect it has on the mental as early as 8. This reason being, with the world we live in based around material objects and money, most inner-city children parents can't afford the latest gadgets when they actually come of age and identify with material items as success. If a child grows in a home where he or she does not receive those things, the child will start to compare their situation to others within the community. If others are receiving the latest tech gadgets, and fashion, he or she will look at themselves as less fortunate. Looking at yourself with shame and embarrassment because your clothes and shoes are not new, nor are they the latest fashion will eventually affect a child psychologically he or she is always aware of how people are perceiving them. As years go on and the child that sees themselves as less fortunate will eventually show behavior issues in school. The ambitious parent, She works hard to supply her child with all the latest gadgets and clothing. Mainly clothing that are overpriced and advertised by rappers and drug dealers, which become the main form of social influence. Children pay attention to their current situation and take note to the jewelry and clothing advertised by rappers, and in return, because it is not the norm to have doctors, lawyers, or any prominent law-abiding career-oriented people encouraging our youth, they will eventually succumb to the environmental factors around them. Take into consideration Paterson N.J., local rap star fetty wap, who recently gained a place in the music world, and a very prominent one. Recently he recorded a video at eastside high school in Paterson in which he also attended. In this song he glorifies his success by stating that school is not a priority, and kids should not focus on school, but whatever it takes to survive our conditions.

Basically stating, welcoming a life of crime, because he feels as though there is no other option.

This is part of the developmental aspect of understanding the influential factors that contribute to social cognition. Do we blame fetty wap, no we do not, and he is also a victim of circumstances that places black at the foot of despair. He too is part of the results of double consciousness. This despair transgresses into a mental processing and will become the social norm.

Mindset in our environments. Youth identify success with looking up to athletes, and entertainers. Why is this? Is this done purposely since inner city youth lack self-consciousness, and are constant victims of double consciousness, which in return leaves room for media and social influence? This media and social influence that is consist of the glorifying of drugs, weapon, sex, crime, and money. If the depiction for a child relies within the hands of our own black entertainers, whose fault is it then, do we still blame white America? Artists have a choice in the music they chose to promote and send out. Is it that since America is a capitalist country and money is a necessity, along with most artist coming from the environments we are discussing

At present, it is clear how they can conform to this way of delivering their message. The message, what is a message, a message has influential ways to affect a person emotionally or get them to think about a current situation that has placed them at odds. Messages are words that one can identify and feel empathetic or sympathetic to. The message is key, and that message has affected and caused the increase in the destruction of our youth and communities. Most will say, people have a choice, and that is right, but what about an 8-year-old black child that does not have a choice in what his society depict for him or her. If the media display black men and women, yelling, screaming, fighting, and committing ignorant acts, all in the name of Gucci, farrago, and other expensive designers that blacks choose to support, what will the child that does not have the proper developmental family structure within the home, father nonexistent, and mothers to stress with work, bills, and school to be able to nurture all elements. What will he or she become? "In New York, in 1925, 85% of kin related black households had two parents." (Walter William June2005) When Moynihan discussed and pointed out the detriment to the black family in his 1965 report, he spoke about the destruction that would soon affect the black community. As the years progressed on from 1925, the decline within black family structure began to pummel. By 1991, the single parent rate for black families was 68% single parent, and in 2010, that percentage increased to 72% of black babies born to unwed mothers. (Washington, Jesse july2014) in a recent census, 67% of black families are single parents with no father present. In comparison, 25% white are born to single parent homes, 42% Hispanic, and 17% Asian Americans. Looking at the statistics provided by the census bureau, it's apparent that nationalities all across the board are being affected by single parent homes, however does all groups suffer from the same social conditioning? No, absolutely not. Even though Asian

CRIME & REASON: A BLACK CHOICE

Americans, whites, and Hispanics suffer from single parent homes, the social influence
is different, as well as the culture. When looking at social influence, we must look at the
environmental factors. The underlying factor is poverty; poverty will affect any ethic
group. Unfortunately, black, and Hispanic poverty differs from white and Asian American
poverty. Black poverty is isolated, meaning it spills over into the community. It plagues the
streets, and it affects the schools also. Families that are white and in poverty, the majority
lives in decent areas, and attend decent schools. Sociologists consider blacks in poverty
suffer from a double burden, like double consciousness.

Taking into account the above information, let's focus on the developmental aspects
that take effect in the home that aids in the social and psychological development of a
community. The two central points of discussion are poverty, and single parenting. Single
parents in poverty with no father assistance fall within government poverty thresholds. In
2010, 27.4% of black were living in poverty. Most of the homes within the threshold possess
inadequate financial stability which in return affects the children in the home. According
to the federal government poverty guidelines, poverty consists of one person making
fewer than 12,000 a year. Now let us take into consideration minimum wage which is 9$
an hour at present, which equals 17,280 a year. Not to stray away from the topic, but while
we're here, let us break this down. Minimum wage jobs are for young teens, and college
students. Most teens with jobs that consist of minimum wage are usually for them to have
some spare cash while attending school. An adult that is working for minimum wage 90%
of the time, they do not possess more than a high education, G.E.D., or none of the above.
The underlying factor is evident, lack of education plays a role in poverty. This fact can
be proven by looking at other nationalities in poverty that are far worse than blacks in
America. Some 3rd world countries suffer from militia groups and governments that control
every aspect of their life. Looking at the aspect just spoken, let us make a comparison.
Looking at poverty in countries like Jamaica, Africa, and some other Caribbean areas,
we can see their conditions are far worse than ours. Take into consideration a family from

either the above mentioned migrate to the United States, within the 3rd generation of being

in America most have established business, education, and homeownership. Shifting to

blacks in America, we are slowly watching our communities destruct, and still oblivious to

the economic plan that needs to be devised. Looking at the facts, both families come from

poverty? Both lack finances and education to obtain a place in the world, however, in time

one begins to progress while the other stays stagnate, or slowly becomes worse. If poverty

or social inequalities, along with social injustice are the real reason behind our situation,

how does a family come over from another country, subjected to the same social situation,

possibly worst; progress beyond someone that has been here all their life. My theory is as

follows, most that migrate, usually migrate collectively, meaning the immediate family

comes over together, the structure that exists within the home remains present. Looking

at most men that come over, they have old world custom, meaning the man worked hard

and took care of the family. What is evident is that poverty is not the only reason for our

circumstances, lack of proper nurture throughout the developmental stages is very much the

blame. This gives you the visual perspective into what is taught in the house will eventually

spill over into the community, and that will then be the social norm for the said group of

people. This is factual because all ethnic groups live within the same communities. By

living in the same communities, the overall perspective of the group becomes the social

and psychological process. Simply put, if the community consists of middle aged white

married couples, the majority are college educated, career oriented, or have some type of

generational wealth. If this is the element of this environment, then the children become

a product of the environment. This is prevalent with the majority of people that migrate

to the United States from poverty-stricken environments. Yes, the criminal element is

present within all groups, but my focus is always the majority. In Maryland, you can go into

some suburban areas and see beautiful, manicured lawn and well-kept homes occupied by

married black couples, with educated backgrounds, and possible military background. As

years' progress on, the children take right after the environment they live in which consist of educated, and married blacks that hold some type of job working within the government. Analyzing the inner cities that are filled with crime, what differs from the black community that I speak about in Maryland? It is the mentality of the people. Yes, we can factor all the elements of socioeconomic status, and social stratification; however, neither of the two prevents anyone from getting an education. The purpose in discussing the above is to show that within the black community, some elements of conditioning can be eliminated with education. Our children are not being taught properly within the homes, along with not receiving the proper nurture needed to develop self identification, and the importance of education. All successful families teach the importance of education and hard work to the children as early as 4 or 5 years of age. The developmental stages are where we develop our characteristics, and social understanding behind what has been seen before us. If a child sees his father constantly working on cars, he will identify with hard work. On the flip side, if a child sees drug dealing as a means of survival, and the proper parental guidance is not present, you as a parent leave the child with room for his or her thoughts to progress on its own. Reflecting upon everything just mentioned, it is possible to say that the developmental stages of a child depend on the social influence of the parent.

The child has no say in what is placed in front of him to interpret. He or she will form their own understanding of the situation, which will play into his psych if the child. For example, a single mother that is in constant relationship abuse is displayed in the house. The emotional level of a child that witnesses this, and can't defend his or her mother will eventually develop Post Traumatic Stress Disorder. Situations like the above cause children to develop anger issues. If issues such as the above are constant along with the other multitude of social stressor, is it relevant why some many black men result in a life of crime. What instills during the developmental stages of development will determine the outlook socially and the influence the environment will have on the particular child.

Chapter 11

Cracks in the pavement

Look for me in the whirlwind or the storm.

Marcus Garvey

With light of the social and developmental aspects that affect the communities within the inner city, one must question what happened? What happened, when we look back, it's evident that the black family structure was much stronger then than now. Unfortunately, every cause has an effect, and that effect can affect a multitude. As stated, in 1925, 85% of black family structure consisted of dual parenting. As years progressed, we watched a steady decline in the family structure. What caused the decline? Looking back over the 20th century, we can name prolific and prominent figures that died with honor, and their name attached to a greater cause. When we look at prominent figures that shaped the consciousness of black America, a list of great men and women shall be mentioned. The shaping of black consciousness revolved around an era of great thinkers, and scholars alike. Through the up rise from slavery, right into Jim Crow. Through vigorous turmoil, and constant oppression, black schools of thought began to emerge, and blacks were now attending some of the most prestigious universities in the world. Armed with a formal education, and emotionally charged to take a stance against racism, and injustice, time were changing for the better in some eyes, unfortunately things became worst for others. As the century turned over, black movements were now being established and armed with educated, intelligent men, and women. Notably members that contributed to black consciousness are, W.E.B. Dubois, Martin Luther King, Elijah Muhammad, Malcolm X, Marcus Garvey, Ida B Wells, booker T Washington, Maya Angelo, the entire Harlem Renaissance Movement and the list goes on. These modern-day prophets spoke words, and display actions that instilled hope and aspiration where there was once clouds and constant thunder, the sun was beginning to shun upon African American with a new identity to recognize with. Whether one agrees with either of the above doctrines, is not of an importance, the important matter is these were men and women that stood up and took the time to invest in its people's consciousness. What they all had in common was they were educated and had an objective for their people, even with them having their own objective as well. Through the words spoken from the great people mention above, there knowledge and intellect gave birth to a new found conscious that the negro was able to reconcile with. The new development of black intellect gave birth to the radical 60's. black consciousness perspective was to help young blacks growing up in a racist country gain an identity into culture and a moral system that was taken away. During the time when these prolific figures were alive and breathing, black families were on the rise, regardless of the circumstances they were faced with. The ambition behind their purpose would mold a consciousness that would live throughout eternity. Looking back at when most of them were born, it was during a time where the black family was the only importance, and the betterment of their current condition is what motivated most through the triumph and tribulation they were enduring. Education was the most valuable element that was implemented within the homes. After being deprived for 100's of years of the right to learn to read and write, blacks took pride in education, and stopped at nothing to obtain it. At the turn of the 20th century, the education that was being taught within black homes began to sprawl into the public's view. By the 1920's, black were making a strong conscious approach toward the betterment of their people. This information was being heard across the world in many different forms, from music, poetry, writing, and art. The 1920's was the birth of the Harlem renaissance era. The era was the opportunity for group expression toward civil rights, black from the south began to migrate north, particularly Harlem which attracted a large group of intellectuals. The Harlem renaissance didn't only appeal to blacks, white was also influenced by the era. This was one of the first opportunities black had that displayed freedom of speech. The birth of jazz established itself in Harlem with blacks migrating from the south. Jazz was a representation of black thoughts progressed into music, jazz was a symbol of freedom to black artists. The era began to fade after the prohibition, and great depression, however, its mark would hold a place in history. As we read through the text, one should identify with the progression of black up from slavery. With black family structures at 85% dual parenting, we can see why the progression for black at this time was prominent. As the years moved on, great movements for the greater cause began to evolve. The N.O.I., The U.N.I.A., and the p African movement. These were not just movements; they were a school of thought that began to awake the consciously dead. Activists promoted and voiced their ideologies with assertion into redefining black place within the western hemisphere. Analyzing the time, why would the times of now be worse for black families in comparison to the early 1900's? blacks at the time had a multitude of social issues, segregation, lack of adequate education, K.K.K., police brutality, Black Wall street, poverty, unable to vote in the south, and a strong deal of mental abuse and inferiority. At present, the injustice, opportunity, and social equality is nothing in comparison to the condition blacks endured at the turn of the 20th century. Analyzing the time is directed toward gaining an understanding into the dynamics that created the social dilemmas that plague present day conditions. The important factor to define is, in 1925 85% of black homes consisted of two parent homes. In 1991, 67% of black family structures were single parent, and in 2010, 72% of black families were single parents. For such a drastic negative turn around, black homes went from a positive 85%, to a negative 67%. What could have possibly taken place between 1925-1991 for this drastic change in black family structures. When we focus on a specific era, we look within the 66 years that the decline began. Analyzing from the 20's and the thirties, this was a time of the renaissance, which was one of the most prominent times of black history. Intellectual black was sprawling up all over the world. Between the 1900's and 1940's, black were enthusiastic to learn, read and write. They enjoy the fact of being able to obtain an education, when at one point, they were denied these opportunities. Moving into the 50's, in the 50's, blacks witnessed another migration, this time some families were moving north without the father present. I can speak for myself, as I go into this element of time, I am able to look within my own family, with my aunt Ella Mae, and both my father and mother's mother, moved north with just the children. Looking back on the first migration, the majority, possibly over 85% of blacks that migrated from the south were two parent families. Evidence shows that in 1925, 85% of black family structures consisted of two parents, so it is safe to say, the percentage that migrated were still two parents. Next, we had another great migration that came about during the 50's and 60's. by this time black family structure dropped from 85% two parent, to 72% In the 60's. from 1925-1960, black two parent families dropped to 72%, 13% less than 1925. What was strange also, was that between 1960-1964, black two-family structures went up 4% to 76%. The most detriment era to black existence outside of slavery is 1965-1991. Most will probably disagree, unfortunately it still will be a detriment, since while the family structure within black communities is breaking down, the violence and poverty is increasing. The current issue that is being brought to existence shows a direct negative correlation. That correlation is as follows, as family structure breakdown, which is a positive, brings forth a negative which is poverty and increased violence. The reality of this matter shows how, in a 26-year span, black family structure that consisted of two parents, dropped an enormous percentage to 68 percent of black children who were born in single parent homes in 1991, according to census.26 years, 26 years it took to dismantle the black family structure. At the brink of it, one should wonder, what could have transpired this detriment? "By the 1960's, American society was riddled with a generation of "white guilt". In reaction a repentance sparked by Dr King nonviolence, civil disobedience and the systemic introspection of the social norm by whites." (dean Kalahar2014). In the article, Kalahari theory states that over compensated entitlement programs based on Johnson "war on Poverty", may have assisted in the start of the dismantlement of the black communities. His perspective insisted that society turned a blind eye to accountability, and from that black began to feel entitled at all costs. This entitlement cost the nation dearly. By becoming, and developing a sense of entitlement, one will utilize the victim stance to justify their action. Justification becomes psychological once an individual places all their bare necessities on a system geared to handicap them. Was it geared to help them or was it a way of giving blacks assistance based on guilt? I say handicap, reason is, by becoming enabled, the accountability factor is now irrelevant. One common issue in black communities that hinder the growth and development is denial. Most would choose to deny the fact of denial; this is common amongst the older individuals in a community.

Chapter 12

social programming, the calm before the storm

Free your mind and the rest shall follow

When we look at social programming, it is defined as a set of instructions each of us learned to fit in with society; our environment, school, home, and social influence contribute to the social factors that define social programming. Programming is symbolic to computational input that is stored in the data on a desktop. That data remains there until it's removed. Our brain processes though just as a computer does. We store and revisit information that is of importance. In communities that consist of violent disturbances, and constant psychological abuse, social programming will become the most prevalent psychological factors that are computed, then stored in our brain. Unlike a computer, the things we store are emotional past situations that were traumatizing or detrimental to your well-being, domestic abuse, and situations that cause our psych to self-reflect, and revisit the situation on a common basis, or when it presents itself again.

The situation that we revisit most from our past, has been the situation that has delayed developmental timely growth within our developmental process. The process of social programming begins with two aspects, mental and physical. The mental and physical aspect co-joins to bring about the social environment. The mental and physical aspect of the social environment is developed through the developmental stages, which brings about the social cognition and perception of a group. When groups or cultures are concerned, depending on the mindset, the understanding of a social environment is first to learn how one thinks. Thinking produces thoughts that develop our consciousness, our consciousness is how we think, the awareness or perception of something. We know from reading that blacks have a double consciousness, and by possessing a double consciousness, social influences are more prevalent within our communities. Social influence is the mental processing of a group that contributes to the social factors of a social environment. Social influence can be good or bad, just look at areas that are poverty stricken, and violence ridden, the social influence is not good. Focusing on an environment, for example an area in prince George's county Maryland consist of educated middle class people with more than likely some military background. What would be the social influence of the children of that environment years to come. More than likely educated, and military officials unless the family structure breaks down and new social norms are implemented in the environment. I use this example to identify with the psychological thought process of a group. Looking at the black nation as a whole, let's focus on the mental and physical aspects of the social environment that contribute to social programming. The mental components of social programming are developed during the developmental stages. If the home produces components that plague the environment, the developmental stages of the child will develop their social cognition from those components. Mental components vary, they can exist with religious belief, radical ideologies, stereotypical behavior, denial, low self-esteem, and so forth. If the most influential person in the home possesses any of the above, the behavior will transfer over into the children. Eventually the children will take the parents' thought, and perception on life, to bring about their own understanding. All this is done while possessing a double consciousness. An example, a 12-year-old child travels to Maryland, and sees nothing but manicured lawns, different from his Paterson environment he just left, his words are as follows, "I don't want to move around all these white people." What develops this concept for a child from a poverty stricken environment that doesn't consist of a white population.? More than likely, he attends the school, churches, and other social gatherings in the community that consist predominantly black, why would his mental perception be interpreted like this. A clear example of social influential processing, these are none other than thoughts of the adults in the environment. The mind is a sponge that absorbs information, the mind at birth is pure and not infiltrated with corruption, without taught the proper understanding, the mind will form its own understanding. The case in many of these homes are single parents and filled with social stressors from the surroundings. Children that lack proper nurture suffer from this, parents that are indolent, will allow the social component into the home, while the ambitious parent spends too much time working and schooling that the children begin to develop the social cognition based on what is seen around them.. This is done by way of social influence. The physical components consist of poverty, and lack of adequate finances. With most children within these homes suffering from this dilemma, media, and social influence will play into the children's psyche. It starts with rap music, which promotes the social stressors of the environment, draws familiarity with the child and their situation, causing the child to begin to idolize that individual whose music relates to their struggle. Children in inner city environments that suffer from poverty, and the inability to afford proper attire, those physical components will develop low self-esteem, Antisocial personality behaviors, and confidence.. Considering all that was stated, when the mental and physical component assist in establishing the psychological process, the outcome of the said group will conform toward the majority. The reason for this conformity, is mere social influence

Due to lack of adequate parenting. Social programming is placed through these stages before its developed. Once the mind has been conformed to the same systematic belief, you will then watch the environment change. So, what changed the environment? From reading we have discovered that in 1925 85% of black family structures were two parent, and economical black were moving forward. Fast forward to 1960, black family structure had fell to 72%. However, from 1960-1964, black family structures climbed to 76%, gain a 4% increase. Then we enter what I call the dark age into black consciousness. From the year 1965-1991, black family structure went from 76% two parent structure, to in 1991, 67% of all black families were single parent. The dark ages into black consciousness is a 26 years' process that flipped the total population into a dark future.

Chapter 13

Triple stages of darkness

If we don't make earnest moves toward real solutions, then each day we move one day closer to revolution and anarchy in this country. This is the sad, and yet potentially joyous, state of America."

~ Louis Farrakhan

The enormous plunge that black social setting took over the 26-year span between 1965-1991 had a few factors that contributed to this down trot. Black homes were 76% two parents. Within the 26 year dropping to a negative 67% single parent homes within the black community. The late sixties brought about change within the black communities. There was a feeling of rejoice as black shouted "I black and I'm proud." Fist were thrown signifying unity and black power which stood to unite the total population of the darker race. This was an element in black history where black began to gain confidence and were able to work and provide an income. In most major cities, black occupied some businesses, even though most were owned by Jews, Italian, and so forth, however, black did possess some businesses, and this was a symbol of moving forward. Black began to remove themselves from white custom and began to embrace their blackness. Afro's were worn by men and women as they gracefully moved through the world with their head high, and fist even higher. Black were now a few decades into gaining education and knowledge of themselves. Some were becoming homeowners, and sharecroppers. With black obtaining education, and advancing in the world of art, music, writing, and sports, they were now getting away from the slave mentality. By 1965 black were displaying self-consciousness and began wearing traditional garbs like their African ancestry. This was a direct result of the effect of two parent homes versus single parent homes. This new emergence of consciousness was being instilled in the homes, streets, and schools. Currently, black display a vast amount of courage, and humility. Black were able to rise through all the hate, racism, discrimination, beaten, lynching, involuntary servitude, rape of their mother, sisters, and daughters. Up from the roots of slavery, right into Jim crow, still I rise. Jim Crow implementation was a mere ploy that caused black to engage in voluntary servitude, for the same masters they were once enslaved to. Still I rise. Through Jim crow, K.K.K., lynching, lawful injustice, racism, and brutal murder, still I rise. The 20th century showed the strength in the black family, this was evident by looking at Tulsa, ok 1921. Tulsa was a tragedy, but God was miraculous working, cause soon after came the most influential history of the 20th century, in reference to the black family. This period was the Harlem renaissance. Black occupied every square inch of Harlem, and the renaissance was in full swing. Legendary figures such master composer Duke Ellington, the great Langston Hughes that travel the world displays his god given talents to multiple cultures across the world, from Europe, Africa and Asia. Langston Hughes book, "wonder as I wander." Gives an historic account of how the rest of the world sees blacks in America. Notably musicians, and writers such as Zora Neal Hurston were part of this great era. This era trickled down into the decades to come, with notable organizations headed by educated and intellectual men. Garvey's U.N.I.A. The movement was gaining momentum and black were partaking in his ideology. In the south, you had the S.L.C.C., and the N.A.A.C.P. The birth of these organizations helped shape black consciousness, and helped them develop a sense of self identification, and pride. As we move into the 40's, black are still maintaining the family structure, as well as moving economically through the system. Considering all the obstacles at these particular times that blacks had to cross. Jim Crow was in full swing, and segregation seemed too prevalent. Through the midst of it all, subjected to worse conditions, still they rose from the crack and flourished. Understanding the time, one would have to identify with a multitude of stress factors that were implemented to start the decline of black families. Looking at the text, we can understand why black were rising in education and the industrial world. The family structure played a part. The part family structure played was the establishment of a moral and value system. As we move into the sixties, a train of events occur to decline the growth of blacks, this process began in 19965-1991.

Chapter 14

Part one: the 50's

You can't separate peace from freedom because no one can be at peace unless he has his

freedom." -Malcolm X (Speech, Prospects for Freedom)

All rights not civil, and all laws not just

During the 50's racial turmoil was at an all-time high. The NAACP witness a slew of its membered murdered by KKK, and racist white mob. These murders were not just African Americans, there were whites that were murdered by whites. What is interesting is, whites being killed by other whites, for standing up for blacks shined light on the situation, and from that we were able to identify that all whites did not feel the same way. The 50's made way for groundbreaking civil rights laws. Blacks were winning the battle in the courts, and the NAACP made it their business to stand up against the south. The NAACP members weren't afraid when it came to the racist south. The racial temperament was increasing, NAACP member were killed and lynched as they made their mark in the south. Lynching was at an all-time high, so was the killing of blacks by civilian whites that would go unpunished. The racial tension increased with the overturning of laws; the south could feel themselves losing the grip they had for over 100 yrs. It wasn't just race based; it was economically based. The south had the agriculture, tobacco, cotton, and other profitable resources slaves worked night and day picking. These white families in the south profited of the back of the slaves, their family wealth was built of slaves, and through Jim Crow, they were still able to implement racist laws that kept blacks from advancing. Civil rights attacked the white south economic and political system, this fueled their anger, because blacks were now owning their own land, and had their own crops that they were able to sell. White American from the south used violence as a tool, and as the civil rights bills passed, this limited what the KKK, and white mobs were able to do to blacks. The 50's gave rise to racial tension. As time passed the mentality of blacks drifted into a revolutionary stance, which was set to take action. The west coast adopted an east coast ideology to further combat the ongoing racial discrimination and prejudice that was being employed by the police force. The west coast had seen an influx of migrants from the south move west; both black and white were migrating. The racist element that existed in the south made its way out west. Blacks out west were victims of police brutality, oppression, and police injustice. During the 50's the racial tension was high, and increased going into the 60's. Laws were changing and civil rights were won. The element of white America that wanted to keep blacks as their tools for economic purpose did whatever was needed to embed fear, and oppression in blacks. The police violence during the 1950's-1970 grew, especially in the larger cities and in the south, a new wave of racist laws, policies, and institutions would be established. The prison population began to increase, and the prison became filled with blacks. On the west coast, blacks, and Latino's occupied the prison walls. The prisons were a direct response to the passing of the civil rights bill. One would have to look at the time frame in which everything surrounding this time came into play. Between 1970-1995, states everywhere began to grow their prison population. This was not only the implementation of the new Jim Crow, this was all based on an economic plot to keep cheap labor flowing in America. The passing of civil rights was in all be all to some, to other's it made matters worse. Malcolm and the nation opposed this, and this was one of the things they stood against. The nation of Islam promoted segregation and stood against the civil rights. After the civil rights (The Act outlawed discrimination based on race, color, religion, sex, or national origin, and required equal access to public places and employment, and enforced desegregation of schools and the right to vote.) Passing, we have learned of the things that took place. One of the most detrimental to blacks was the steady increase in the prison population. "In qualitative terms, California began the 1970 as home to the nation's most progressive correctional systems. From world war2 through the early 1970's, under democratic, and republican governors, California approached a precedent based on rehabilitating prisoners. Starting in the 70's California shifted toward total incapacitation." (J Simon2014). The 50's would be the years in which the pot began to brew, as we moved into the 50's, out of the 40's, there were a few things transcending. Blacks were now a few decades out of slavery, and we were fighting for equal rights. During the 50's racial tension soared. This tension was wrapped in racism, and violent out lashes by mobs of whites. Lynching was in full swing, and in the 50's everything would come full swing. "The Southern states account for nine-tenths of the lynching's. More than two-thirds of the remaining one-tenth occurred in the six states which immediately border the South: Maryland, West Virginia, Ohio, Indiana, Illinois, and Kansas."4 Mississippi, Georgia, Texas, Louisiana, and Alabama were the leading lynching states. These five states furnished nearly half the total victims. Mississippi had the highest incidence of lynching's in the South as well as the highest for the nation, with Georgia and Texas taking second and third places, respectively. However, there were lynching's in the North and West. In fact, every state in the continental United States apart from Massachusetts, Rhode Island, New Hampshire and Vermont has had lynching casualties."

With lynching going on for at least 60 years by the 50's, black families would face a generation of inferiority by way of the KKK, and white mobs. Fortunately, blacks learned to live without fear, and when the 50's came in, they began challenging the laws that were created with prejudice. The NAACP began their fight in 1951.

Chapter 15

Part 2: Civil rights movement

"Darkness cannot drive out darkness: only light can do that. Hate cannot drive out hate: only love can do that."

- Martin Luther King Jr.,

The 50's marked the time of racial turmoil

Up until 1954, blacks in the Americas had never dealt with white America equally, before Jim crow, it was slavery. Blacks in the Americas identified with white America as the oppressor, and people of power. This in return established the inferior element in blacks when it came to deal with white America. So many black during this time were killed by the hands of whites that in time it ignited a radical stance from the inner-city blacks. Up from slavery, right into Jim Crow, the embedded fear that was implemented during slavery still coexisted once the slaves were free. To keep this fear instilled, groups such as the KKK and the black legion were created to keep the fear alive.

Jim Crow kept blacks as a resource for white wealth. At this time whites were blacks' landlords, employers, governors, senators, president, and oppressors. Blacks worked for whites, got paid by whites, and owed a portion of their checks to local stores for food by the time they received their check. The quality of the food sold to the colors were of a lower grade than that of the white, and a lot of the colored only places were owned by white. So instead of black's money circulating through the hands of their own, the money circulated right back into the hands that paid them. Cheap labor has always been America's most prominent resource, segregation was just a ploy to keep blacks as a resource and in 1954, this ever so present evil that loomed the sky's in the west was coming to a head, and it was raising the radical element here in America. As the pot brewed, the racial tension increased, and the oppression became political, and psychological.

Jim Crow was finally defeated in the court of law. The first case that challenged the Jim Crow laws was Hernandez v Texas may 3, 1954. In this case, the supreme court ruled that

Mexican American and all other racial groups are entitled to equal protection under the 14th amendment "All persons born or naturalized in the United States, and subject to the jurisdiction thereof, are citizens of the United States and of the state wherein they reside. No state shall make or enforce any law which shall abridge the privileges or immunities of citizens of the United States; nor shall any state deprive any person of life, liberty, or property, without due process of law; nor deny to any person within its jurisdiction the equal protection of the laws."

This case broke the mold for many cases to come. 2 weeks later May 17, 1954, the brown v board decision was finally in. This decision would change the climate in America to come. New political strategies and economic ploys to keep blacks within the confines would be soon implemented. Brown v board was the supreme court ruling that declared segregation within public school unconstitutional. This supreme court ruling would increase the racial tension and white America would fight to keep segregation prevalent. Multiple situations rose from the brown v board, with the supreme court defining segregation unconstitutional, and being the highest court in the country, white America didn't feel compelled to follow the ruling. Another case was Davis et al v the St Louis housing authority which would end discrimination in public housing. These three court cases were just the beginning of multiple supreme court rulings, and civil rights laws that would be implemented. In response to Rosa Parks and the Montgomery bus boycott, November 13, 1956 Gayle v Browder would end segregation in intrastate travel. One supreme court ruling that would create a deeper racial tension was the, June 12, U.S. Supreme Court in Loving v. Virginia strikes down state interracial marriages ban 1967. This was the last supreme court ruling of this time. The rulings above set the racial tension in America. With blacks, soon to gain equal opportunities, white America felt as though this would affect the economy, and white southerners would do everything in their power during this time to keep segregation alive. The presidents during this time would have a heavy influence on decisions made in support of black America. President Eisenhower, Kennedy, and Johnson assisted the civil rights movements. These decisions would begin a turmoil and increase the racial existence that exists within the west. Political decisions increased the racial tension, and violent tempers began to flare for both sides. As the decision came down, the police force became more aggressive in urban areas. Police violence against blacks during this time was atrocious. Not only did blacks endure police brutality, they also suffered from white violence committed by white American citizens. The supreme court rulings would force the KKK and other white supremacy groups to hang up their robes for police uniforms. Between 1950-1970, the black community would endure a slew of murder leaders,' by the hands of whites American. Vicious acts were committed, and children and mothers were beaten, or killed during this period. The supreme court decision that was granted gave blacks hope for change for the better. Jim Crow had finally came to an end and Lyndon Johnson would pass the bill prohibiting race discrimination of any sort. The ever-present inferiority that was embedded during slavery was now beginning to cease. Black organization between this time frame was sprawling up all over the country. These organizations were aimed to uplift the black community and restore a sense of pride within the hearts and souls of black folks. Young blacks geared the information with college literature, and revolutionary intelligence. As the 60's roared in, so did the new black. The black power movements. These movements restored black consciousness, and made blacks embrace their natural beauty, and the term" I'm black and I'm proud became a household slogan. This was the response to the inferiority leaving the soul of black folks. Unfortunately, just as decisions were being granted by the supreme court, there was an evil countering these decisions with vicious acts against black's. one that would strike fear in blacks in Mississippi was the innocent murder of Emmitt Till. Two white men charged with the crime are acquitted by an all-white jury." His assailants–the white woman's husband and her brother–made Emmett carry a 75-pound cotton-gin fan to the bank of the Tallahatchie River and ordered him to take off his clothes. The two men then beat him nearly to death, gouged out his eye, shot him in the head, and then threw his body, tied to the cotton-gin fan with barbed wire, into the river." They later boast about committing the murder. Emmitt Till was savagely murdered, the two white men had no compassion for the boy, there compassion didn't exist, his skin was brown. Multiple act of crime was committed against innocent blacks exercising their constitutional rights'. 1955 On May 7 Reverend George W. Lee, an NAACP activist, is killed in Belzoni, Mississippi, 1951Harry T. Moore, a Florida NAACP official, is killed by a bomb in Mims, Florida, on December 25. 1959. On April 26, Mack Charles Parker is lynched near Poplarville, Mississippi, 1963 On June 12, Mississippi NAACP Field Secretary Medgar Evers is assassinated outside his home in Jackson. The deep-seated evil that existed In white America was not a condition of all, but the energy that came from the south was sinister. 1964On June 21 civil rights workers James Chaney, Andrew Goodman and Michael Schwerner are abducted and killed by terrorists in Mississippi. "The racial terrorism ranged from cross-burnings and churchbombings to beatings and murder. In the summer of 1964 alone, Mississippi journalist Jerry Mitchell reports, "Klansmen had killed six [people], shot 35 others and beaten another 80. The homes, businesses and churches of 68 Mississippians associated with the civil rights movement were firebombed." With black's freedom of speech, and the civil rights movement gaining momentum, there would be a price to pay. N.A.A.C.P. witnessed multiple members killed by the hands of white Americans who did not agree with the chain of events that were beginning to evolve. Civil rights activists took their fight to the south, and in return, lives were taken. Angry white mobs took the laws into their own hands, and whether wrong or not, they were acquitted of all charges 97% of the time. This keeps the inferiority in blacks. The justice scale was unequal, and blacks would get the short end of the stick. Countless murder went untried with no conviction, and some even slide under the rug. To be of a group that does not feel the sense of security from your own law enforcement, would cause traumatic stress in the environment, and these stressors would bring about a radical stance. Black American feared coming across an angry white mob while traveling alone. This fear was already a genetic predisposition passed down through DNA. Through the generations, each generation of black Americans would have this same inferiority that was present 200 years ago. Most situation involving angry white resulted in death by way of lynching or beat to death. In the south preferably, there was a deep-seated racism within all power structures. White America counter black opportunity since the reconstruction era and beyond. "1966 On June 5, James Meredith begins a solitary "March Against Fear" for 220 miles from Memphis to Jackson,. He traveled Mississippi to protest racial discrimination. Soon after crossing into Mississippi Meredith is shot by a sniper." States like Mississippi, Texas, Alabama, Georgia, Louisiana, Tennessee, and North Carolina housed the most KKK organizations. The states also had the most lynchings', with over 500 recorded. That deep inferiority that existed in blacks in the south would also migrate up north during this time. "1963 Four young black girls attending Sunday school are killed when a bomb explodes at the Sixteenth Street Baptist Church, a popular location for civil rights meetings. Riots erupt in Birmingham, leading to the deaths of two more black youths (Sept. 15)."1968 On February 8, three students at South Carolina State College in Orangeburg are killed by police in what will be known as the Orangeburg Massacre." Senseless murders after murders, and increased police brutality was becoming a social problem in black America. The collectivistic culture that once existed within the black community was now becoming severed through social injustice policies. Freedom came with a price, and the price was not adding up. Blacks were gaining a political stance but losing tremendously socially. Homes were burned, churches were destroyed, and innocent men and women looking to be identified as human for once were killed for it. This was beyond economical, this was a hatred, a deep hatred, that has yet to be understood. As the civil rights bill passed, racial tension increased, and the evidence was clear that blacks were still second-class citizens. The murders and lynching that occurred during the time of desegregation, caused traumatic stress within black America. The hopelessness that they thought would fade, was still present. Psychologically this affected the black population because it opened the doors for individualistic cultural development.

Chapter 16

Riots and Radicals

One ever feels his two-ness – an American, a Negro; two souls, two thoughts, two unreconciled strivings; two warring ideals in one dark body, whose dogged strength alone keeps it from being torn asunder.

W.E.B. Du Bois (The Souls of Black Folk)

The years to come for black families would soon face atrocities that would cripple the race. 1965 marked a year for a turnaround for black America. Going into 1965, one would think things would become better since, between 1960-1964, black families had a 4% increase in two parent homes. 1964 marked a good year, with DR King winning the Nobel peace prize, as well as influencing congress to pass the civil rights bill, which meant everyone would be treated equally. This was a prominent moment where blacks were maintaining family structure, and work. Unfortunately, the civil rights bills didn't change much, blacks still were deprived of equal opportunity, or no opportunity. With good things coming to pass, there was also an element brewing that would affect the black population socially, and psychology. As 1965 came in, black community started to take a different approach toward the injustice they were receiving. The emotional level of blacks was now becoming impatient, and their behav-iors began to display it. Blacks began to become emotionally irate. The poten-tial emotional build up would soon spill into the communities, and affect those same communities' generations to come. On august 11, 1965, this emotional irate energy would soon unfold, causing the Watts riots, were 34 people died, 1,032 injuries, and 3, 438 arrests. 34 deaths are a tremendous amount of blood shed. Unfortunately, rioting is the biggest form of protest expressed by the black race. Not only was it a protest for humanity, it was a voice bellowing from the pits of the race that would only speak out with vengeance. The riots were a devastating blow to the already damaged inner cities. The Watts riot incited due to an African American motorist who was pulled over for drunk driving, and a fight broke out, in which the driver was brutalized by police. Blacks at this time in L.A. began to feel the same pressure that was placed on blacks in the south. With the influx of southern whites moving west and began occupy-ing the L.A.P.D. The racist element began to increase out west. This led to the watt's riots were 34 were killed, and over 40 million in damages. Who would agree that the 34 deaths who were more than likely predominantly if not all black, that this was a strategic move to take a stance toward social injustice, and social inequality. I disagree with this form of rioting, reason being nothing was ever accomplished, it only set the black race back. However, the under-standing is clear why it occurred, it was the only stance blacks could take that would be heard. Unfortunately, it was a foolish act on our part, simply because all businesses and homes that were destroyed were in the communities. Some of the businesses were black owned, but the majority were not. riots proved to be more detrimental than beneficial, economists state that in all cities where riots took place, the median of black family income dropped 9% from 1960-1970. With the percentage dropping, this meant more blacks were displaced with work, and forced to indulge in a criminal element. "considering the wave of race riots that swept the cities from 1964-1971, there were more than 750 riots, killing 228 people and injuring 12,741." (Virginia postrel2004) What was not recorded in this study was the amount of black were displaced from their homes due to the fires, and the destruction of property. Major cities felt the wrath of riots, Watts, L.A., Paterson N.J., Newark N.J., Jersey City, Chicago, Detroit, and a host of others. Looking at it from a statistical correlation, as the riots incited, the property values, and labor went down, while the crime, single parenting had increased, until present day, the effect is, black on black crime; which is more common in all areas where there was a riot in the 60's. The riots were the direct result of long time suffrage and police brutality. The riots were one element that contributed to the downfall of black family structures. During 65-75, the temperament within black communities began to change. The thoughts that contributed to shaping black consciousness were now becoming old, and being replaced with a new allegiance to the black situation in America. That new allegiance would spark a radical chain of events with the intention of restoring blacks' proper place in humanity. It was now being dis-played by sports figures, actors, and actresses. Black were now representing themselves with the raise of the black fist, which enticed black power rhetoric. This rhetoric was being adopted from a socialist and communist approach. With the birth of the consciousness, which consisted of African American tak-ing a leftist approach toward capitalism, gave birth to the black panthers. The black panther was a strong voice in the community at this time, they were geared to protect blacks from racist cops that patrolled the streets of Califor-nia. Just as there was a great migration of blacks moving from south to north, there was also a great influx moving south to west. Two of the founding mem-ber's families had also migrated west from the south, Bobby Seale, and Huey P. Newton. Armed with a radical rhetoric, shotgun, and an understanding of the law, the panthers were now taking a stance against police brutality. not on-ly were they taking a stand against police but also the political situation that inner city blacks were facing. The black panthers chose the emblem of a panthers as a representation of what happens once that panther is cornered, this logic was similar to what black were enduring at that time. Black panther branches were popping up all over the country, in all major cities, the panthers were establishing food drives, free clinics, and multiple necessities that assisted blacks where they were being deprived. This new rhetoric that was being im-plemented were falling on the ears of the inner-city youth, and now transform-ing their consciousness in a more radical approach toward white America. As this new approach gained notoriety and proved at the time to be very affluent in black communities. Unfortunately, as this approach was gaining media attention, what was steadily declining was the black families. Not only were the black families declining, but statistics state that approx. 25% of first generation blacks were born to teenage single mothers. By 1980 this number was at 31%. The mere fact of the matter is that, between 1965-1975, not only were the two parent structures breaking down, but a new element was imple-mented into the equation, and that was teenage pregnancy. This moment marked a spike in the cultural perspectives of blacks. As teen pregnancy went up, single parenting also increased. Teen moms were none other than the children of the single mothers. This was a clear demonstration of the effect of single parenting, the first element from this particular problem results were teen pregnancy, and soon another element that would deliver the crucial blow to the black family would be implemented. As the temperament grew within the black communities, so did the criminal element. Analyzing a F.B.I. Uniform Crime Reports, which displayed the worst years in crime as a whole. Between 1962-1991, murder went from 8,530 to in 1991 24,700, rape 1960-1991 went from 17,190 to 109,060, assault 1960- 154,320, 1991 1,135, 610, burglary, 1960, 912,100, 1980-3,795,200, and vehicle theft 1960 328,200, 1991-1,661,700. Evidence shows how from the 1960's to 1991 not only was the black families decreasing, but crime participation was rising. With crime rising, in-carceration became the new social norm within the inner city. Looking at the corre-lation between the two years, the evidence is clear, as to when the criminal el-ement began to invade the minds of the inner city. As the criminal element derived, new sub-cultures were beginning to pop up all over the country. By 1975 black had witnessed over 750 riots within the inner city, police brutality, and the demoralization of character. Looking at the information that is present, we have learned over a 10-year span, black families began to become dysfunc-tional, and multiple stressor were now being implemented on top of the ones that were already present. The mentality of blacks began to take an emotional ride, with the history of slavery, right into Jim Crow, black began to feel hope-less. This would be relevant being that as we were freed from slavery, the in-tention was grandiose. Unfortunately, the hate that was embedded within a strong percentage of whites was still present. That presence keeps black infe-rior; it has almost become a mental phenotype within the black's percep-tion. Why do we develop this concept so young without even understanding the world we live in? Can this play on the mental perception of our youth due to the fact that this energy that displays our inferiority is as if it's embedded in our souls? Do We naturally or genetically conform to inferiority?

Chapter 17

Part 3: the birth of the sub-cultural influence 1965-1975

Too many so-called leaders of the movement have been made into celebrities and their revolutionary fervor destroyed by mass media. They become Hollywood objects and lose identification with the real issues. The task is to transform society; only the people can do that

Huey Newton

A subculture is defined as a cultural group within a large culture. Within criminology, subculture theory consists theories that argue that certain subcultures in society have values and attitudes that are conducive to crime and violence. by the late 60's, the inner city was witnessing a cultural influence that would shape black America for the next generations to come. Just as we enter in to the 70's, the birth of Bloods, Crips, Vice Lords, Gangsta disciples, folks, P stone rangers, Latin Kings, and 5% came into play. Also a host of other small sub-groups that isolated in one or two particular areas, such as the M.O.V.E movement, B.L.A., and the sons of Malcolm X.

As these sub-groups began to populate, they began to cause a split within the black communities, and at this point is where the raising of the fist was beginning to fade. With the birth of the sub-groups, marked the birth of black on black violence. We know that violence against each other has always happened, but not to this magnitude.

The subcultural was what began to separate the blacks within a community, and years to come this element would soon surface full force. With the black communities dwindling by the year, the black panthers also began to dismantle. By 1970, the B.B.P. had established 68 branches in 68 cities. their influence within the black community had gave them a heroic image, and blacks all over were embracing it. There radical stance was gaining the mentality of the youth, and the deep-seated hate that had produced over the years was now being developed into social cognition of inner-city black communities. With the riots placing black in an angered state of hopelessness,

CRIME & REASON: A BLACK CHOICE

Youth conformed to organization and sub-cultures would take the influence of mental processing for the years to come. The youth that soon conformed to this way of thinking posed what I call radical hate by way of emotional attachment to the situation. With history constantly reflecting on the negatives that blacks faced, which is more than the positives. Blacks develop a fail first mentality because society, and media has labeled them unintelligent and not equal in humanity. The depiction of the riots, slavery, lynching, and police brutality is constantly reminded to blacks. From this depiction, black can develop post-traumatic stress due to constant imagery of negative depiction. As generations progress the more they think in this manner, and it will soon have some effect on the total population. If blacks are constantly reminded of the negativity that has been endured, and when the information is given, whites are at the end of every sentence, this will develop inferiority, and a depiction of being less than. Once our minds begin to except this concept, one can find him or herself hating and discriminating against someone from a different ethnic background they have never met. This is prevalent in all races, not just black and white. Not to mention, it's evident that blacks started to see education as less of importance, and work as a demand; with that in mind, there was a high level of illiteracy, and lack of proper education. Without education one's mind is able to be manipulated by social information produced by a socially influential group within the culture. If that influence is negative, but counter a person's emotional interest, without proper education going in, one can be utilized in a manner more destructive than constructive. If the influential members possess a high level of knowledge within a subject, and attach the emotions of a group where they are predominately uneducated, and possess a double consciousness, they're liable to conform to what most peers are conforming to. Social information is the most detrimental when utilized by the wrong hands. Looking at social information, one cane sees how the radical element began to affect the inner city. Just look at variables discussed, in comparison to the year before the decline, we can now focus on the issue at hand. The issue at hand will give insight into the real reason behind the black population's way of thinking. Social information during the sixties changes the consciousness of black America, for what appears, from a statistical point as the reason for the change came by way of influential factors during 1960-64, and progressed up into 1991, and present. it's evident that the mentality of blacks changed during the 60's, and with that change came the decline of black families, and consciousness. That change became apparent by 1975, sub cultures were now occupying the corners, with what initially started as a revolutionary tool, would soon succumb to the social stressor that came by way of the riots, and began focusing on the criminal element. As the riots transgressed through all major cities where there were predominantly black populations, the property value, and labor decreased due to jobs relocating. When work becomes scarce and you lack the necessary tools to obtain a job other than industrial, one will result in means of survival, and that's preying on the environment. When members of a cultural group begin to prey on the environment, it implements a new stressor within a group. Take into consideration how Bloods and Crips and other gangs began to progress through the 80's, the violence that was committed against each other was atrocious. This violence began to be inflicted in the house, and by the 80's domestic violence in urban cities was taking course. With the radical stance taking the minds of the youth, this created a progressive antisocial personality disorder in black youth. Let's reiterate the facts, as we know through a F.B.I. crime report, that between the 1960's to 1993, crime increased tremendously. While crimes increased, so did the incarceration rate. With the incline in the incarceration rates, came teen pregnancy. The dysfunction within the homes began to penetrate, and with only one parent available, the outside environment became the home environment. This period would affect the overall mental health of blacks, and with stricter laws geared to dysfunction black homes, mothers were left with no direction.

Chapter 18

Part 4: sub-cultural effect

Nobody in the world, nobody in history, has ever gotten their freedom by appealing to the moral sense of the people who were oppressing them.

Assata Shakur

Between the years of 1975-1985, there was a brand-new element being implemented within the black community, with the years 1965-1975 bringing in radical change, and revolutionary concepts, the masses began to take a more violent stance toward injustice and inequality. The stance triggered a series of riots that resulted in millions of dollars in property damage, and a decrease in labor. The decrease in labor by the end of the 60's shows through a correlation, the increase in crime. With blacks unable to obtain work, the increase in burglary, and vehicle theft began to triple over the years. Also, during the Vietnam war, there were 525,000 troops deployed to Vietnam, with a large percentage of the troops being black. This was crucial to black family structures that weren't financially frugal, to lose a male a within the family marked a decline in the finances. With the Korean war ending in 1953, and the Vietnam war began in 1955, and ending in 1975. An influx of black was admitted into these wars. Most blacks recall family members coming back from the war with drug addiction, and P.T.S.D. From a psychological standpoint, a large percentage of black males came back from the war with concurring behavior. Co-occurring behavior is the prevalence of two addictions, that's a mental disorder, a substance abuse working at the same time. Blacks were coming back from war to deal with injustice, inequality, and lack of work due to discriminate. Large percentages of black males returning with this condition, and lacking adequate finances to afford mental health, most black fell into a state of depression. Black coming back from the war possibly suffered from P.T.S.D., substance abuse, and depression. The P.T.S.D. and substance abuse developed from the war, and depression developed from the condition they were subjected to upon their return from the war. It was like Langston Hughes dream deferred. Blacks that assisted in the winning of the wars, felt as though they would return and be accepted not as a nigger, but as a patriot. However, nigger was still the mentality that was present in the inner city. Looking at this from a mental perspective, envision, you fight, and place your life at the tip of death for a cause you really have no clue about, but you take this stance with the intention of now being identified as someone instead of something. Black felt by participating in the war this would solidify their space in America. To come back and not receive all that you anticipate, along with staggered unemployment, and lack of job security, the mental reflection will eventually emotionally affect the said person, and that emotion will define his character, personality, perspective, and views of the world. This may be why so many war vets joined radical militant groups such as Black Panthers. The 60's marked the era of the rise of the radicals turned leftist. War vets that joined these militant groups possibly had personal vendetta against the government due to the response they received coming back from the war. That emotion is what ignited the fire behind the black power movement. Emotionally charged with a radical theoretic, the 1960's produced the element of a hate relationship with whites. This hate relationship, which clashed with white hate, resulted and assisted in the decrease within the black communities. The radical element proved to not be as effective as most thought, the end results are present now, which will be addressed in later chapters. As black power faded, a new vanguard was awaiting to take center stage. Subcultures became very influential between 1975-1985. The west coast would feel the wrath of this new birth in black inner city. West coast black who survived the 1960's faced even more social dilemma, the birth of the sub-cultural effect. Bloods and Crips began to flood the inner cities of Los Angeles, these sub-cultural groups took the influence of the communities and conformed most of the youth. As we moved into the 80's, gang violence took a shock wave effect over Los Angeles, the violence became a plague within the communities. Drive-by shootings were occurring randomly, and black on black crime was increasing tremendously. As gang violence became the face of California, urban inner cities areas that were affected by the riots, and police brutality by way of the L.A.P.D.

soon made way to gang culture. By 1969, Crips began to emerge followed by bloods in 1972. As of March 1992, out of 942 street gangs that were identified through the G.R.E.A.T. system, 299 were classified as black street gangs. With these forming as a protector of their communities from police brutality, soon they began to assist the police department in the destruction of the black families. By 1983, both groups had spread throughout Los Angeles and began to establish their organizations funding through criminal activity, removing any positive motives that once existed. Blood and Crip gang violence increased as the years went on. The war between both has resulted in an unknown amount of black on black deaths. As we move into the years 1975-1985, teenage pregnancy is up to close to 50%, and single parent homes at over 60%., and black families are declining at a rapid rate. Black youth were conforming to gangs as early as 13 years old and being introduced to a life of crime by 14. Bloods, and Crip have developed an image within the United states as violent criminals with antisocial personality disorders. This image has caused social influence within the community, and the youth have begun to identify with gang conformity as the social norm. recruitment for both gangs by the 80's had begun to spread out throughout the community. Each group began to break down into subsets. Each subset took on a new identification under their particular gang. Ex. Rolling 60's, 20's, 30, and kitchen Crip. These are all Crip organization that occupy different territories in L.A. the same concept applied to Bloods. With the drug trade increasing, so did the violence. The violence started to become internal, Crips began to go to war with rival Crips, and bloods also began to take this turn. As the west coast went from the black power movement to Blood, and Crips, the east coast was experiencing a different transformation. The emergence of the 5% nation of gods and earths began to invade the minds of the inner city. Just as the 5% were increasing, so was the Muslim population. East coast families began to convert from Christian to Muslim, or 5%. New Jersey is a good example of this transformation. Inner cities such as Atlantic city, Newark, and Camden families converted to Muslim between 1965-1975, by 1985, these cities were predominately Muslim, either Sunni, or N.O.I. Cities such as

Paterson, Jersey City, and Trenton became predominantly 5%. However, all surrounding cities became influenced by one or the other. New York, and Connecticut also experienced a major influx of 5%, and Muslim conversion. With the outlook of both set on positive affirmation in righteousness, unfortunately the criminal element also became very influential to some members. A new division within communities on the east were occurring, Muslim, and 5% shared conflicting views that eventually created tension. Muslim didn't agree with the 5% ideology, in which they identify themselves as Allah, which Muslims took somewhat offense too. As the 80's transformed into sub-groups, a new element would be implemented which would cause a great deal of violence. With the 80's came crack, crack was the answer to inner cities resident's financial problems. Once the drug influence entered the gang realm, murders began to increase, and sets began to war over territory. Black on black crime increased just as the incarceration rate. As the new social elements become implemented, the stressors from the past are still present. Not ten years out of the black power era, the gang era took completely over all inner cities across the world. As gang population increased, so did the murder rate. Teen pregnancy by this time was an all-time high, and single parenting was increasing tremendously. Young black males, the majority, would eventually enter the drug trade as a means of survival. With poverty, inadequate housing, drugs, violence, and lack of education, one can see why youth that have been developmentally delayed from living within homes that consist of drugs, and domestic violence would take this road. As the drug trade entered, so did hip hop. Hip hop stood to restore the thinking of our youth Artists delivering positive messages that influenced the importance of education, hip hop was becoming the emerging voice for the black community. Unfortunately, by 1991, hip hop took a different face. The music began to glorify, and almost praise the violence within the communities. The promotion became a very influential element in the black inner cities. By 1995, most positive and conscious music was replaced with the glorification of drugs, guns, killing blacks, and disrespect to women and the community.

Chapter 19

part 5: warring ideology

Dr. King's policy was, if you are nonviolent, if you suffer, your opponent will see your suffering and will be moved to change his heart. That's very good. He only made one fallacious assumption. In order for nonviolence to work, your opponent must have a conscience. The United States has none.

Stokely Carmichael

As the 1950's roared out, and the 1960's roared in, there were two warring ideologies that would affect, and split the black communities. Looking at the media's iconic black activists, Martin Luther King, and Malcolm X.. The media gave a great deal of exposure to these two, in which it caused a split within the communities. Both theories were geared toward the improvement of the black race and its position in society. Malcolm x concepts on the black issue in America, and his rhetoric distinguished from the ranks of the Nation of Islam. Founded in 1934, the nation of Islam stood on principles of black nationalist, with a religious overtone. The black national concept of consciousness ignited the radical elements within the black community. The black nationalist ideologies gave birth to a new consciousness with the developmental aspect of black consciousness. The new development changed the social climate within the communities. The principles that governed the nation of Islam stood on segregation. The nation of Islam was geared toward blacks developing their own social environment without the assistance of what to them are consider white devils that seek to destroy the black race. The dynamics of the nation of Islam stance is the total acceptance of embracing your black culture and identifying with your ancestry root, instead of the ideologies that were inflicted by white America during slavery. Nation of Islam awakened black consciousness through a radical perspective that brought about change in the communities. However, not until Malcolm x evolved did the nation begin to gain media attention. Malcolm x became the front spokesman for the nation of Islam, his voice carried across black communities stating what the rest of the population feared too express. Malcolm X's famous quote changed the dynamic of urban society. Malcolm x spoke adamantly and blatantly toward the American government that inflict social injustice on the millions of minorities that lived within the U.S.Looking at Malcolm x life and early childhood, one can identify with his fiery aggression that he so adamantly displayed in his speeches. Malcolm had something that most men couldn't identify with. Malcolm X emotional charge was a rage and anger that would develop into what we recognize today. 1931, at the tender age of 6, Malcolm lost his father, not only did his father die, he was killed in the most inhumane way by the K.K.K. Malcolm's father was a devoted follower of Garvey, which was implemented in the household, along with being a Baptist. The black nationalistic approach was already embedded in Malcolm, unfortunately, the trauma that he would endure from his father's death would be the passion to spark a movement. Understanding the dynamics of the developmental stages of development, we can look at Malcolm x situation to gain an identification into the man beyond the media depiction. Losing his father to the hands of white supremacy Malcolm harbored the disdain for white America due to the traumatic issue that occurred with his father. He knew not how to express it nor was he intelligent enough to articulate it now either. Upon his incarceration, he would come to grips with something that he could finally express the pain he struggled with all his life. Malcolm got introduced to the nation of Islam, and quickly embraced it. Malcolm didn't embrace the nation with his mind, he let his heart make the decision. He was lost, and vulnerable, and becoming part of the nation not only gave him an identification, but it gave him the chance to express the pain he felt from losing his father. The rhetoric of the nation of Islam gave insight into the psychological element he faced and endured. As the words of Elijah Muhammad echoed in his ear, and the resentment he expressed toward the white race catered to Malcolm emotional stance with white America. He became passionate and honored to stand and fight against the injustice that killed his father. The Nation of Islam seen Malcolm as a charismatic figure, and placed him were black population was dominate, Harlem. As Malcolm rose to ranks, so did the notoriety of

CRIME & REASON: A BLACK CHOICE

the nation, during this time Malcolm had major influence on most blacks that conformed to the nation of Islam. His prophetic fire gave the youth a self-identification into what it means to be black. Malcolm preached that all blacks should get rid of Christian customs and adopt the nation of Islam. He advocated segregation and advised black to take a radical stance against injustice by any means necessary. The youth gravitated to Malcolm's delivery, because it addressed all that most blacks feared to stand up and say. Malcolm was speaking for everyone. This voice fell upon the minds of the socially illiterate, and emotionally uneducated. This mixed with the physical elements that blacks were enduring which would soon spark a movement which would be called the black power movement. Malcolm became the face of the nation, and behind his exposure, the nation would soon get its place in the media. Malcolm gave rise to the nation, eager to serve Elijah Muhammad who took him out if the triple stages of darkness that he once was subjected to. Malcolm embraced the nation with loyalty because he felt revived, and as if he had a purpose beyond what he was used to prior to incarceration. His self-identification became clear once he accepted the nation of Islam. This was a self-identification that identified with the suppressed traumatic situation he endured at the tender age of six. Malcolm was a devoted Muslim, and student of Elijah.

Malcolm was not only dedicated to the movement he was also determined in growth and evolving of his character.. He seized the moment and faced his inferiority while speaking from his gut. It was a much-needed stance within the black community, however the interpretation delivered on death ears without totally understanding can result in a detrimental situation. As an adamant advocate of socialism, and nationalism, Malcolm theory upon what was needed from black started with the undoing of white culture that was implemented during slavery. He constantly pounded the rhetoric of the white man as the devil and boasted the fact of how blacks should arm themselves. Malcolm talked with disdain about Christianity and its origin. He believed that the religion of Christianity was a brainwashing tool designed to keep blacks inferior and under their rule. The nation of Islam believes is separation, and that there should be no integration. This stance was administered to the communities, and it went at their heart and soul. The pain that was felt as Malcolm delivered constantly the epitome of slavery, and psychodynamic destruction it did to blacks, it invaded the sub-consciousness of blacks, and eventually attack the emotional element. The emotional element mixed with factual base, fueled the anger that created the black power movement. Soon enough, the media exposure would subside with the agenda, and the new agenda would be to eradicate Dr. Martin Luther King. Malcolm's constant ridicule of Dr. King began to invade the minds of the youth, causing the new generation to pick an ideology. Malcolm x constantly and publicly devalued Martin's theories, principles, character, and honor as a black man. For the masses, this would carry on, and Malcolm took center stage with his delivery that was deliberately done to shift the followers of King, who were Christian oriented, and spiritually based. The ploy established was to constantly pound into black America head the origin of how Christianity became a religion of blacks in America. The nation displayed images of slavery, abuse, racism, hatred, and overall abundant of facts that blacks should identify with. This was indeed a fact, I believe that blacks should be well understood into their origin, and the path that was created to separate them from it. The history that was removed from the minds of blacks was much needed going forward into the improvement of our condition at that time. This rhetoric gave insight into the beauties of being black. It gave us our place in history. A place that was replaced with a history that was not our own. Malcolm utilized this with the fact that still to present date, black were still being treated inhumane and discriminated upon. Malcolm's charge at police brutality only ignited the pain he now understood that affected him from his father's death. Police brutality amongst blacks was none other than K.K.K behind another badge. His identification with the issue dealing with police discrimination, and police brutality mirrored his emotional components that developed from his traumatic stress behind his father's death. This rage mixed with hate based theoretic triggered a change in how black conceptualized their situation, on an individual basis that formulated into a majority based.

CRIME & REASON: A BLACK CHOICE

By attacking Dr King's position amongst blacks, Malcolm caused some to choose sides. His word, Malcolm states, "the reverend Dr martin Luther king is subsidized by white folks, white pay dr king to implement this passive behavior amongst black folks so they can stay under the white man rules." Statements and words like these change the complexity in the communities. Once blacks became conscious of how Christianity came about, and information in reference to their position during slavery, some start to question Dr. Kings position as if it was only geared to suit his benefits, and not black. Malcolm attacked the religion of Christianity once he began to speak in the manner he did, it caused a split between the older and the younger generation. The older generation belief and value system was structured around a Christian base. Malcolm x constantly criticized the Christian religion, and ridiculed Martin Luther King at the same time. This was a perfect strategy of divide and conquer. Malcolm X speech traveled to all major city, preaching Islam as it was taught by Elijah Muhammad. The Nation's goal was to increase their ranks and become a focal point in society.

As Malcolm ridiculed Martin over his views, perspectives, and religion, Martin chose not to retaliate with a response, only clearing his views from what was being said. King was humble in his approach, and his views nor did perspectives change from beginning. He went in with the non-violent approach, and went out with the same views. King was a man of vision; his vision was before his time. Prophetic in his own way, king new no color lines. From being a devoted Christian, king administered love with his persona, and his deliverance. King was passionate within the quest for civil rights, unlike activist in the north, activist in the south were faced with more consequence from southern whites, than northern activist faced from northern whites. Kings persona would soon be recognized by the world and accepted by all men and women no matter race, color nor ethnicity. King was dedicated to total change across the board for the betterment of social equality and justice for all ethnicity. Many radical activists criticized king theory which was based of Mahrati Gandhi. "Gandhi saw violence pejoratively and also identified two forms of violence;

passive and physical. The practice of passive violence is a daily affair, consciously or unconsciously it is the fuel that ignites the fire of physical violence". Gandhi was opposed to violence because it opposed hate. Just as Martin did when he formed his movement. Martin studied the approach to American injustice, and applied Gandhi theory which was utilized and deemed effective. Martin non-violence civil disobedient approach to racism in America was effective and gained the media attention it needed to lift the cover of America and the discrimination against blacks. Dr. King created and fought for civil rights and was able to obtain great responses to the black condition, and discrimination. King concept would test the moral integrity of woman and man, for one that could stand and watch someone get brutalized, lynched, hosed, bitten, and demoralized as a human being. The non-violence method triggers a vast amount of white supporters. The non-violence method would cause a division within the white community, this division would cause whites to look at their neighbors in a different light. King's peaceful protest was almost a cry out. Dr. King had faith in his vision, and King knew that all whites did not feel the same way. King knew if he could use this form of protest, he knew he would be able to publicize to the world that white men and women were fighting for civil rights of black also. By publicizing the matter at hand, the world would then look into their moral character, and if they come to grips that they are not part of the percentage that are aim to destroy, eventually they will conform, and join, or voice their opinion from a far, had they chose not to identify with the wrongdoing of blacks. As we moved into the 60's with the younger generation changing from the moral and value that was established in a household from the 1920's through 1960's. The two warring ideologies were crucial to black consciousness, therefore creating a split between the homes, forcing social influence to raise and develop the mentality of the youth to come. Martin and Malcolm were two prominent figures in the black community during the civil rights era. The thoughts and words of these individuals would spark the consciousness of blacks for The years to come were similar in what they wanted but different in some.. Malcolm looked at physical elements that would be needed to be implemented for change to develop. Malcolm's by any means necessary was to change the climate within the black community. This statement ignited the fire that sparked the black power movement to stand up and fight whether it be mental or physical. Malcolm's theory differed then martins, and neither of the two elements could work at the same time, the division would cause a split, and those that disagreed with Martin's non-violent approach would eventually conform to Malcolm's. Looking within both individuals, we can define the psychological factors that contributed to defining their character. Both came from different backgrounds, and animosity was different toward whites due to this. Understanding the developmental stages of development within a child, we learned that two parenting is effective, and nurture is most necessary for the proper developmental of the individual. At the age of 6, Malcolm lost his father to K.K.K. members. The traumatic effect of how his father was killed, and why he was killed would affect his developmental process to come. Malcolm's life mirrored the image that black in the inner city develop at present date. Lack of a father present, along with multiple siblings, the finances of the home would dwindle. Malcolm watched his mother struggle while venturing into the world and identifying with race elements that plagued black communities. With education being scarce and no father presence, the level of conscious development lacked, and forced the social environment to be Malcolm's social cognition. Identifying with blacks as white saw us, Malcolm conformed and searched for the success that white obtained by becoming a criminal. Without the prevalence of education, the streets raised Malcolm, and from what he endured while in the streets, and the traumatic stress of his father's death, and his mother's struggle would define his character, which would soon result in his incarceration. Upon his incarceration, like so many black men, this becomes the first time they actually begin to process their thoughts, and how they think. Countless hours spent alone, one only has the option to think. This thinking produced thoughts in Malcolm that wanted answers. He began to search and educate himself. While incarcerated, and possibly at a point in striving to identify with himself, he is introduced to the nation of Islam. At this point in

Malcolm's life, while being incarcerated he processed his condition and the condition of his people. While gaining insight into the condition of his people, he also had to reflect on his father's situation and counter it with his conditions now. Anger began to seep, and the nation of Islam was the perfect factor to be placed in front of him at that time. Even though Malcolm doesn't possess an educational degree, his father was a Baptist preacher and an advocate of Marcus Garvey. These images would be the only identification Malcolm would carry of his father, and those images would mold his thinking with his own experiences. Malcolm wanted change, he wanted to become something other than what he was representing at the moment. Malcolm knew he was doing everything against his father's will, and he sought out to change that. With Malcolm's father being removed from the home, the foundation was swept from up under them. The Christian element that was implemented through slavery, was what the slave carried with them into freedom. The thoughts of most slaves were that the emancipation proclamation, and the freeing of slaves was the one of many prays answered. Black moved out of slavery with the clothes on their back and the bible. Even knowing the concept behind religion, and the identification into what it was initially utilized to instill, black had developed and interpreted their own concept of the bible and God. The morals and values that were instilled from the bible would create structure in the family. Christianity was the dominant religion in black households. Blacks had no other religious understanding nor strong conscious belief into their true identification. They took the important element out of the bible and attached to the emotional elements they were faced with throughout slavery. The important elements were what administered the importance of family and providing food, clothing and shelter. Blacks took the bible and utilized it to gain an identification of who they were. With this element being removed from Malcolm's home, it left the family no foundation to stand on, and once the foundation which would be a Christian upbringing has been removed, the social influences of what blacks were subjected to would become their cognitive development. There were no other forms of religion prevalent at that time. Malcolm journey into Islam was the answer to all the question he kept concealed throughout the years, Malcolm wanted a change and that change came in the form of a rhetoric that would allow him to address his father's killers. Not the actual killers, but the system that created the killers, institutionalized his mother, and dismantled his family. At the tender age of 6, he witnessing the atrocity that he had and forced to survive without any guidance, the Nation of Islam gave him the structure and identity he needed to become a better person. Malcolm embraced the nation with honor, and loyalty. Malcolm made a vow to be loyal and to rid his body, and mind of any poisons that would hinder his growth. He was taught the history of the black race in America, and what established their identity here. They taught Malcolm that Christianity was the white man religion, and that schools that he built are only for his people. These thoughts and concepts of the Nation became his own, and Malcolm became one with the nation. Without an identification, he became what they wanted him to be. He was intelligent, well read, witty, and charismatic. Those years of incarceration was Malcolm rebirth into society. Once Malcolm was released the nation embraced him. Note, most incarcerated men that go in with nothing, and come home the same will appreciate the simple gesture into assistance. That assistance that Malcolm was embraced with, would sustain his loyalty and honor within the nation. Malcolm was obedient for he felt that without the nation he would be back into the streets again. This loyalty matches his now trained aggression toward whites along with the traumatic issues from his father's death, Malcolm's persona and deliverance was what the nation needed. When we look into Malcolm's chronological timeline, we can see the social cognition that develops the mentality of children that suffer from dysfunctional homes. Malcolm's father was killed in 1931, at the tender age of 6, by 1939 at the age of 14, Malcolm's mother was admitted into a mental institution, leaving Malcolm in foster care. Between 1941 and 1946, Malcolm's life would finally meet the destructive pattern that is so common in young black men today. The prevalence of this situation is so common with the condition of blacks, that the radical element is a multitude of social stressor that becomes a perception of an individual's everyday thought process. Those stressors implemented with a conscious response, and without the proper education behind specific subject will result in a bias, prejudice, and discrimination. These results come from emotionally attaching to the subject, and only identifying with the conflicting issue, versus the generalized issue. This means from Malcolm's experiences in life, he socially developed a passion to hate whites from a multitude of factors that played into the equation. The attributes that contribute to his disliking had become part of his automatic thinking. this would be common, due to his chronological representation. Malcolm's most emotional moments in his life up until this incarceration had developed his deep hatred for white America. Most possess this but won't admit due to denial, and taking the victim stance. While incarcerated, everything Malcolm read or learned he used to develop a hostility toward white. What is deadly about obtaining an extensive amount of knowledge charged with a hatred, and emotional attachment to the social condition that you are passionate to address, one will develop a biased perspective toward anything other than his or her belief. This showed in his delivery when attacking Martin Luther King. He criticized his religion, education, and political stance because it wasn't one with his own. Instead of sticking to the generalized matter, Malcolm chose to attack the most personal matters. Upon his release from incarceration, Malcolm heads to Chicago to live with Elijah Muhammad. Within one-year Malcolm becomes the minister of temple 11 in Boston. After one year in Boston Malcolm is then moved to Harlem's temple 7, and one year after he is then moved to Philadelphia. From an east coast perspective, Malcolm's influence became heavy within large urban communities that consisted of a poverty-stricken environment with racial tension between blacks and police. His words cut through those communities with an identification into the message. These large urban cities that consisted heavily of young blacks, they began to emotionally attach to the rhetoric, even if they never joined the ranks of the nation of Islam. Now let's look at the effect of Malcolm word throughout these areas. Each one of the major cities has a social influence on the surrounding cities. With this major influence, matched with the social condition that black was emotionally attached to, this ideology began to seep into the homes. As it seeped into the homes, it then became the overall social influence of the majority. Looking at what we have learned thus far matched with the power of social influence, as the years progressed and integration hit, the racial tension began to triple, and black became more emotionally hostile toward whites. Black became more emotionally hasty as the physical and mental abuse of particular whites tripled and became much more savagely as integration began to spread rapidly. Not only did black take discrimination from everyday whites, this discrimination became more political as the new elements in black communities which was deemed a threat to national security became more relevant. This mixed with the ideology delivered from Malcolm x thoughts on separation, and the most crucial blow of them all was the religious aspect the nation made it their business to discredit at all cost. Now let's focus on the psychological elements, looking at the black race history concerning the oppression of white supremacy, which consist of hatred, discrimination, separation, not identifying the other in a humane state. The words cut the same and triggered the same psychological effect, nigger, coon, jigaboo, monkey, tar baby, beast, uncivilized, and worst of all not even considered a full man, only 3/5. The flip side, whitey, devil, cracker, and other identification that defame character, will only produce a hate element. The ideologies are the same, just one is geared toward the white race, and the other is geared toward the black race. Even though the comparison is nowhere near equal, whites don't emotionally or internally attach to name that blacks have for them, for they identify with those names being derived from a deep hatred toward the white population based on social factors. On the other hand, blacks emotionally internalized the names subconsciously due to the 100's years of oppression. A black child can identify with being called one of the above names before they are 5 years old, versus a white child probably won't come to grips with his designed name until his teenage years. Black process this discriminatory factors, and defamation of character as early as 6 years old. With that being said, the issues that blacks face with whites are implanted during the preoperational stage of development, therefore attaching emotionally and subconsciously. These result in free flow forms of inferiority. Looking into the psycho-dynamic influence of the situation, the ideology mixed with the racial temperament, only had one reaction, which was riots. This ideology mixed with the racial tension created the riots. History shows prior to, black had been placed in the worst situation that did not result in riots. Let's look at wounded knee, and black wall street along with several bombing, killings, lynching, etc., when the violence and discrimination was worst, why did it not trigger rioting? What was the overall mentality of black throughout 1900-1959? Was it the same from 1960-present? What changed? From reading above we know that poverty affects the community as a whole, unlike white poverty which is more isolated since a large percent of whites are middle class. ThE child will still benefit because of what the majority consists of. Vice versa, in the black communities poverty is a majority issue, so it can't be isolated. With the majority living within the range of poverty, social influence is high. Looking into the riots, and what could have caused them, we must look at the new form of thinking that was being implemented. Focusing on the black power movement of the 60's, prominent activists during this movement were Stokely Carmichael, Huey Newton, and Bobby Seale. The black power movement created its theories and ideology based off Malcolm concepts while in the Nation of Islam. As they became educated, the more they denounced King's non-violent concepts. Could this new mentality that was being implemented be part of the hostility that has been implemented in blacks from the inner cities. The only difference was that the activists of the 60's didn't involve religion in their political stance. However, they allowed the same element that blacks endured from whites, to become their characteristic, and that was black supremacy. On the surface no one would say that they are black supremacists, it is shown in the behavior, the same is what is identified in white supremacy. Looking at the effect of both mentalities clashing can result in a detrimental situation and wage war on American soil with violent responses only resulting in blood shed. During the riots, the majority of the dead were blacks when it was all said and done. who suffered from the recovery of the devastation that could have resulted in waging war against the government? This rhetoric would have only made the innocent inner-city youth the sacrificial lambs. The government would have called in martial law, and poor blacks would have been left defenseless without a chance to fight. This wasn't realistic when we look at the time. Through the late fifties, Malcolm commuted to all major city and changed the thinking, by the early sixties, the youth that had conformed to this way of thinking without joining the nation of Islam would go on to create their own movements. As the words entered the minds, the racial tension rose, and created the black power movement. This form of democracy is detrimental and cannot be utilized to reconstruct the black consciousness. It promotes hate, and advocates physical force, a force that could not have been won through violence. The violent element was the crucial blow to the destruction of the black power movement. This element fell upon the emotional imbalanced and developmentally delayed. Charged with racial hatred, radical attitude, with a lack of full understanding into the matter at hand, the years between 1955-1965, we saw the effect of this. The result was shown in 1965, in Watts, California on June 11. From 1965-1970, 750 riots erupted across the country. Looking at Martin theory which was derived from Mahrati Gandhi, which was non-violence, historical facts have been proven that this concept works. It was proven by the people of India, in response to the treatment of the darker race. Martin took an intellectual approach toward the situation that blacks were dealing with in America. Both individuals were geared to restoration, one was emotionally charged while the other was intellectually and spiritually charged. The emotional aspect is important because it defines the characteristics of the person. This is based on how they attach to issues concerning their needs. Malcolm's history, and his education was racial geared toward black national stance due to life challenges. Martin on the other hand was the result of a stable two parent home that instilled moral and values based on the bible. The upbringing is what separates the emotional intellect. Both faced the adversity that came with the prejudice that was inflicted by whites. Martin's perspective was a southern perspective where the racial tension was triple what it was in the north. Not to say that racism in the north wasn't just as bad, however the south was were Jim Crow held its mark. What separated both was the developmental process and what was endured through the development of each social cognition. Their social cognition differed due to environmental circumstances. And as they moved into teen years, the two represent the direction in which black men and women go today. High percentage of youth in single parent homes result in crime to survive, while children in two parent's homes have high chances of obtaining a college degree. This element exists within the black communities today. Martin flourish in education within the realms of prestige school and obtain a substantial amount of degrees and certificates. Malcolm on the other hand, obtain his education by being self-taught, then taught by the nation of Islam. The important element to understand is, they had different social perceptions because Martin had a diverse perspective while Malcolm had a limited perspective, only seen through the eyes of blacks. Martin was able to see the world with a better vision because the educational process was different. Martin sat in the classroom with other races and understood them socially from a positive and a negative. Martin had identified through his travel that all whites didn't feel the same, and being a god fearing man, in his heart he could only love because this was all he knew, and was taught through his developmental stages. Martin would never conform to a radical stance because history never revealed where this strategy was effective. This was the emotional response to blacks that felt pressured by white America, not to mention the poverty that added to their stress. Most were unable to identify with the issue due to lack of education so they internalized the emotional pain it built, and it progressed between the years of 1955-1965. The new generation became emotionally charged, and the social emotional issues that plagued the environment would soon spread like cancer. This would spread little by little as blacks took note of racism and physical abuse. The feeling of hopelessness, and not an answer into why we are born into these conditions soon affected psychological development. While Malcolm experience for blacks were real and vivid, martin was the flipside to the black homes that maintained two parents and a moral and value system. Martin obtained his doctorate in systematic theology, meaning he was able to become educated and establish friendships with whites that saw no color line, and this would be something that would govern martin's perspective, which would be only right from a Christian standpoint. Martin didn't see fit to condemn an entire race off of what the majority felt. Malcolm felt as though all should be held accountable, and from his social perspective that would only be right due to his traumatic, post traumatic issues that derived from his childhood. The hearts of the two were different, the experiences caused them to see differently, but their objective was to see the betterment of the black race. Looking at the things from Malcolm's view, we can see how his rhetoric, and concepts are what change the mentality of the next generation, from a statistical standpoint, it would actually be for the worst of the black population. Malcolm's death would soon be the cause for the uproar in the black communities, with conspiracies that Malcolm was killed by the F.B.I. caused blacks to develop an even deeper-rooted hate. This time, it would result in a change of events to come. Before his death Malcolm's view and perspectives would change. After Malcolm returned back from his journey to Mecca he began to denounce the Nation of Islam and became orthodox Muslim. Malcolm's new views embrace people of all races and colors, unlike his past views, he was now willing to work with Christian ministry, or whomever was willing to assist in the reconstruction of black America. This new perspective was totally opposite to what he once preached as a minister within the ranks of the nation. There are many speculation into what really drove Malcolm to leave, only one can speculate, most say due to Elijah Muhammad infidelity and adultery, unfortunately Malcolm saw more, Malcolm had rid his self of dealing within anything that represented incarceratio. Malcolm had seen that within the nation their was a criminal element that existed, also Malcolm could have believed that being that blacks in America had not yet came to grip with culture in the east, the nation of Islam was mimicked the orthodox Muslim for their own personal needs. This wouldn't be hard to believe being that blacks only attachment was to their religious belief, and if you could persuade their religious concepts, you then have complete dominance. Is this why Malcolm spoke the way he did toward Christianity while he was part of the nation? There are many different possibilities, unfortunately Malcolm would not live long enough to fully evolve into the new identity. However, the damage had already been done, from the years Malcolm evolved within the nation of Islam from 1952-1964.Malcolm's influence changed the climate within the urban environments, this climate was now part of the radical thinking that transgressed into the black power movement. Malcolm had Influence in Chicago, Boston, Philly, and New York, and New Jersey. Malcolm theory by any means necessary would soon be the answer to the situation in California. His thoughts would be manifested through the B.B.P., the black panther party for self-defense. The party established their format off Malcolm X principle on revolution and taking a stance even if it meant bearing arms in defense. With the recent spike in police brutality in the west, the racial turmoil was at an all-time high in the west. The panthers came to establish self-defense against police brutality. This new movement raised a revolt in America, and within three years it established 68 branches in America. The Panthers would soon be dismantled with F.B.I. constantly looking into them. The panther's criminal element would soon surface, and by the 1970,the panthers strived to take a different approach which was a more political stance. They strived to get away from the criminal element which was called the underground, this movement within the black panthers assisted in hiding individuals that were on the run from the judicial system. As the panthers started to dismantle in 1969 there was the new wave of sub-cultural effect and most fashion their movement behind the panthers concepts that concept became irrelevant as gangs started to increase. Analyzing both individuals, we can identify with who may have had the popularity within the black communities. Malcolm had a great influence in Philly, NY, Chicago, Detroit, and Boston. These were predominantly large cities that would have an effect on the surrounding cities. For example, New York would have an influence over N.J., and Conn. Malcolm's influence would also hit the west coast, but represented by the black panthers. Martin's influence was predominantly in the south. Evidence shows that

CRIME & REASON: A BLACK CHOICE

Malcolm had a larger following consisting of mainly inner city blacks. This generation would be where the riots began. Looking at the influential aspect of words, Malcolm sympathized with his audience. His words created confusion due to blacks possessing a double consciousness and only identifying with God and the bible. Malcolm infiltrated their ear with words that stated that the Christianity was a tool to keep blacks enslaved to the white man. He wants you in his schools so he can continue to brainwash you, and keep your mind and body enslaved. This soon caused blacks to question the belief system that was implemented in the house. Some conformed to the nation of Islam, and most just dropped the religious aspect and adopted a radical perception toward life, and white America. As Malcolm traveled the inner cities professing the word of the nation, it was as if this was a plot to cause a division within the people. Through the fifties, Malcolm X whom with the assistance of Muhammad Ali began to become a bigger influence due to Ali political stance with the war and adopting the nation of Islam. blacks identified with Ali, and Malcolm as the pillars to the black community. With Ali being the heavyweight champion and also speaking out toward racism in America, he began the media spotlight, with Malcolm in tow, vice versa. Blacks in sports were at this time just breaking the color lines. The issue became a national situation. As desegregation swept through America. Violence committed by whites toward blacks began to increase. The increase in violence mixed with the black nationalist social influence, produced a level of hatred along with a new rebellion toward religion and education. for the inner-city blacks, just like Malcolm. The Nation of Islam plan catered to the what blacks wanted so bad, but was afraid to speak on. Malcolm executed the nation Of Islam plan just as anticipated. This would not only awaken the black inner city, it would also divide the black population. In a Malcolm X interview, "he contended that if the leaders of the established civil rights organization persisted, the social struggle would end in bloodshed because he was certain the white man would never concede to full integration." Malcolm's negative demeanor toward civil rights activists was publicized which he did on national TV. This was crucial at this time because black needed all the unity they could get. Malcolm didn't choose to bash civil rights activists privately, but he did it publicly. From the statement Malcolm believed that if the civil rights activists continued to push for integration, it would result in bloodshed due to white's not wanting to desegregate. Unfortunately, there were a large percentage of whites that did push for desegregation. The above statement wouldn't be factual since the element that produced the bloodshed was already present from the trans-Atlantic slave trade. Blacks suffered more bloodshed in the years before the 60's then beyond the 60's, this element was present and still is, however we can understand the concept that Malcolm referred to regarding white America because it has validity to it. The main objective to Malcolm theory was that he was concerned about the angle the civil rights activist was using, which he believed was a hindrance, but he couldn't see the promotion of his ideology on the black race which he was steadfast in arm defense, and bloodshed if need be. This promotion invaded and affected the inner city that took on Malcolm's social views, but not his religion. The nation of Islam seen it fit to promote this new found consciousness amongst the uneducated and emotionally attached. The people that took on the approach, but chose not to join the ranks of Islam, would soon be the ones behind the riots. By any means necessary was a cliché that would depict an image of Malcolm holding a 45 looking out the window. Krs-1 used it on one of his album covers, which was a way to bring the newer generation to grips with Malcolm concepts and thoughts on the black race.

Malcolm concepts spread through the inner city and began to affect the way they depicted white America. Blacks were already on edge since the conditions were beginning to become worse. As the condition became worst, and the social influence of the nation became more prevalent due to Malcolm X and now Muhammad Ali. Their influence took the minds of the inner cities captive. They were folk heroes that were standing up against white America. Blacks conformed to Malcolm's influential rhetoric because he admired his strength and honor. He was a representation of the inner city. Malcolm's influence would spread fast across the country. His influence would override Martin due to the slander

Malcolm used toward Martin, he painted Martin and all the civil rights leaders as bourgeois that were steadfast in aiding the white man in destroying the black race. Malcolm spoke of arm defense to a group of people that was never taught to defend themselves. The influence would spark a chain of events to evolve during the sixties. As interrogation began to take effect the racial tension began to rise. As the racial tension rose, so did white on black crime. As the tension increased so did Malcolm's influence. It was Malcolm who flooded the nation with followers. This division would be detrimental to the black race. As more blacks began to accept Malcolm concepts, the more they began to denounce what was considered the white man's education and religion. Blacks that did not chose to join the ranks of the nation of Islam would soon denounce their Christian background. How this would be detrimental would be shown in the years to come. This generation that detached from the moral system of the foundation of the black race, which was indoctrinated through Christianity now chose to obtain their own knowledge of self. Once the inner city began to take this approach, this brought on the radical element that would unite the black power movement. All key activists during the black power movement fashioned the ideologies of Malcolm's perspective. The black panthers would be the group that would take this perspective to the next level. They practiced arm defense and executed their 10-point program which was devised based on Malcolm's views. The panthers would introduce Malcolm rhetoric to the west coast who would eventually conform through emotional attachment based on their circumstances. This sounded perfect upon the misled ears. Unfortunately, they would be the sacrificial lamb for something greater. The nation of Islam gained popularity of the inner cities through Malcom years . Malcolm was minister for a year each in Boston, Philly, N.Y, and he spent his first year living with Elijah Muhammad and studying in Chicago. By being involved with the conscious development of the black population in these areas, one would also gain the popularity of surrounding cities that suffered from the same social injustice and inequality. Malcolm's influence in the north dominated Martin, leaving him with only the south. Malcolm constantly seemed fit to antagonize Dr. King on national television. He spoke out about kings being subsidized by white America, Malcolm took center stage when it came to addressing the King in the eyes of white America. This would cause the division in the black communities, causing some to conform to Islam, while others remain Christian. With two cultural perspectives evolving amongst one group of people, the outcome would only be a detriment once opinion began to flare. Religion is one form that can get the response from an audience. Malcolm addresses the civil rights activists with a distance, basically separating them from the general issue. Malcolm theory caused black to become biased toward a religion that blacks had come to accept and fashion their lives based on. The bible was the only thing black felt as though they owned. The one thing the master couldn't take was their ability to pray. As this became the moral foundation of the black population due to the fact that the true cultural origin was removed, and blacks had no direct lineage to their birth country. Malcolm attaches the psychological element of the black race. That psychological element was attacking the only thing that black could say they owned, which was the ability to believe in god. Now there was someone from their ranks that was known for telling them that this was the religion of the white man and it was used to trick them into staying psychologically enslaved. Malcolm spoke these words to blacks and they attached to them because they were able to see the effects of what he was saying. By emotionally attaching to the words, it mirrored their perspectives and what they endured from white America on a constant basis. Intellectual thoughts did not omit when the frame thinking became established, emotional response resulted in deeper issues within the community. Looking at the time, it was ripe for the season. When social conditions remain the same for a long period of time, new stressor becomes implemented, and as we know poverty is not isolated in black communities, nor are the social stressor. They affect the community. These new social stressors would soon surface in the communities.

Chapter 20

Malcolm X Vs. El Hajj Malik Shabbazz

"Education is our passport to the future, for tomorrow belongs to the people who prepare for it today."

– El Hajj Malik El Shabazz

When looking at the information presented, we can look at the social influence and how it affects the inner-city community. The condition results in conformity based on the majority. This was the phenomenon of the 60's. as different radical groups began to rise, so did the police presence and their tactics. Malcolm's words ripped through the inner cities at a rapid rate. The passion behind Malcolm's words were felt in and out of prison. Prisoners began to take a political stance with the intention of mimicking and gaining notoriety through community and media depiction. This concept of blacks and media plays into the psyche of most that come from poverty-stricken environments. We can look at the effect the hip-hip industry has on our youth. Lines and violence erupt at local malls and sneakers stores just to receive a pair of Jordan. Most that are buying are living below the poverty lines. Materialistic items that symbolize status entice young black youth with the purpose of looking successful. This is the direct result of a lack of self-consciousness. If one lacks proper self-consciousness, are they vulnerable to social influence? When we look at how Malcolm words created movements that would continue to the present date. These movements consist of the B.L.A., black panther party, M.O.V.E., and the sons of Malcolm X out of Camden, N.J. Harlem, Boston, Chicago, and Newark, N.J. would adopt Malcolm ideology and theory. Unfortunately, most still contend and support Malcolm rhetoric to this day, when that name was denounced for Malik el hajj. The imagery that society depicts of Malik el Hajj is that of Malcolm X. a figure and custom that once was based of the nation of Islam principle had chosen to denounce the name of Malcolm X and become Malik el hajj. Malcolm X's (Al-Hajj Malik El-Shabazz) Letter from Mecca

THE PILGRIMAGE TO MAKKAH

When he was in Makkah, Al-Hajj Malik El-Shabazz wrote a letter to his loyal assistants in Harlem... from his heart:

"Never have I witnessed such sincere hospitality and overwhelming spirit of true brotherhood as is practiced by people of all colors and races here in this ancient Holy Land, the home of Abraham, Muhammad and all the other Prophets of the Holy Scriptures. For the past week, I have been utterly speechless and spellbound by the graciousness I see displayed all around me by people of all colors.

"I have been blessed to visit the Holy City of Mecca, I have made my seven circuits around the Ka'ba, led by a young Mutawaf named Muhammad, I drank water from the well of the Zam Zam. I ran seven times back and forth between the hills of Mt. Al-Safa and Al Marwah. I have prayed in the ancient city of Mina, and I have prayed on Mt. Arafat."

"There were tens of thousands of pilgrims, from all over the world. They were of all colors, from blue-eyed blondes to black-skinned Africans. But we were all participating in the same ritual, displaying a spirit of unity and brotherhood that my experiences in America had led me to believe never could exist between the white and non-white."

"America needs to understand Islam, because this is the one religion that erases from its society the race problem. Throughout my travels in the Muslim world, I have met, talked to, and even eaten with people who in America would have been considered white - but the white attitude was removed from their minds by the religion of Islam. I have never before seen sincere and true brotherhood practiced by all colors together, irrespective of their color."

"You may be shocked by these words coming from me. But on this pilgrimage, what I have seen, and experienced, has forced me to rearrange much of my thought-patterns previously held, and to toss aside some of my previous conclusions. This was not too difficult for me. Despite my firm convictions, I have always been a man who tries to face facts, and to accept the reality of life as new experience and new knowledge unfolds. I have always kept an open mind, which is necessary to the flexibility that must go hand in hand with every form of intelligent search for truth."

"During the past eleven days here in the Muslim world, I have eaten from the same plate, drunk from the same glass, and slept on the same rug - while praying to the same God - with fellow Muslims, whose eyes were the bluest of blue, whose hair was the blondest of blond, and whose skin was the whitest of white. And in the words and in the deeds of the white Muslims, I felt the same sincerity that I felt among the black African Muslims of Nigeria, Sudan and Ghana."

Upon his return from the holy city of Mecca, Malcolm no longer viewed the world through Malcolm X, he was now Al Hajj Malik. Looking at Malcolm plight through the nation of Islam Between 1952-1964, he made one of the biggest influences on the black race. Charged with an animosity that wanted to voice, and have an opinion in the change of blacks, he embraced what he felt would suffice. The nation proved to Malcolm that despite your flaws, and your history, you're a Blackman. The nation taught Malcolm self-pride, and how to stand firm within the eyes of the oppressor. The nation had rid Malcolm of his fear, inferiorities, and insecurities. The nation gave Malcolm his redemption. It molded his characters, views, and perceptions. The nation had given him his birth rights as a black man in America. Defining a consciousness that would serve a multitude of minds for influence. The nation molded Malcolm into what he'd become, without the nation, there is no Malcolm X, nor would there be a El-hajj Malik el Shabazz. Reading his letter is a direct representation of who El Hajj Malik El Shabazz had become, his tone and person was the total opposite of Malcolm X. El-Hajj Malik would take a different approach toward the conditioning of black America, unlike Malcolm, El Hajj was more concerned with the issues on a national scale, after denouncing the nation, El-Hajj would become more adamant to work with civil rights activist nor matter race color or creed. By accepting Islam, El-Hajj began to broaden his horizon beyond Malcolm thoughts. While Malcolm promoted separation, and armed defense, El Hajj focused on integrating for the betterment of the black race, and the importance of letting go of prejudice, and hateful ways of thinking. El Hajj showed growth and development within his new-found characters. The words that he once expressed toward Dr. King, he was now willing to go against. His new perspective of Islam caused him to denounce the Islam of old, and except all races equally without any prejudice. El Hajj no longer looked at whites as the devil, he embraced them as his brothers and sisters. Under two different life changes, Malcolm and El –hajj made a great impact on the consciousness of blacks in America. Malcolm X gave blacks the voice with aggression and demand for change. Malcolm taught black how to face their fears of the white man and how to master their inferiority. Malcolm spoke what most would not. In the eyes of blacks, Malcolm was a hero in their eyes, like that one slave that would stand up and fight the master while the rest looked on with fear. Unfortunately, Malcolm's views were distorted and promoted the same behaviors he was striving to address in white America. The same hate that some whites displayed, was the same hate Malcolm X striving to bring alive in the black. Malcolm was emotionally attached to the situation because the nation catered to the answers that he needed all his life. Malcolm X brought change to the black communities. He was the first of our time that went to prison and came out as he did. He was the knight in shining armor for blacks, he wasn't passive in his approach, he was aggressive, and his words displayed it. as Malcolm changed from nation of Islam, to orthodox Muslim, a good deal of people would soon convert. The cities where the influence was heavy were Philly, Newark, Camden, Harlem, Chicago, and a few other cities. looking at these cities, the population consist of majority Muslim. Before El Hajj El Malik, inner city blacks had no recollection into the religion of Muslim from a orthodox stand point. They quickly embraced this religion based on Malcolm. Within the 60s we watched a vast amount of inner-city home transition from Christian homes, into Muslim homes. The psychology of the situation takes a turn, even though homes began to adopt the religion of Islam, people still was left with no choice but to view his vision from a Malcolm X stand point which was denounced. With adopting the new religion, people didn't lock into his new vision, they stayed within the old vision which was still associated with his past. Malcolm's influence trickled down into generations and perpetuated a mindset that turned into black on black crime. The increase in community organization brought about the difference in opinion and perpetuated the division among African Americans.

Chapter 21

Christianity vs Islam

I believe in a religion that believes in freedom. Any time I have to accept a religion that won't let me fight a battle for my people, I say to hell with that religion.

Malcolm X

Looking at the time frame between 1900-1955 black households consisted of a Christian background. The Christian background was indoctrinated by white slave master. Whites practiced the bible and considered the blacks to be the beast of the earth. This religion was inflicted on slaves by force, until it became embedded. By the 1800's blacks had lost their connection to their customs and origin. By this time generation had been indoctrinated with Christian concepts and moral. The bible was interpreted to blacks as a ploy to keep them psychological enslaved. Whites keep blacks from learning how to read and write, so, for a long period of time black were able to understand the bible, other than how it was interpreted . As the generation progressed on, the connection between Africa and America was far gone. Blacks in America had now conformed and become totally indoctrinated to white customs and religion. Blacks by the 1800's had become emotionally attached to the religion since that was all they possessed . slaves had no choice but to attach to the religion and the omnipresence. Blacks emotionally attached to the religion because they had nothing else that would listen to them cry out their pain. Prayer was the only form of consciousness blacks possessed. They looked to god through prayer for a change in their current situation that they were being born into. Slave communities were establishing Baptist churches of their own. Without being able to read or write black only new the bible and its scriptures. There were no other influential factors within black communities to change the con concept of religion from slavery up until slaves were free. Once slaves were free they keep there moral and values they were indoctrinated with, blacks begun to become preachers and get their own churches. The Christian doctrine was the only influence in the homes and as the years progressed on blacks thanked their new found success of freedom to the many of slave's prayers that were answered.

Black families flourished and began to gain economical success throughout the early 1900's. within the early 1900's there were black organization and movements formulated, but none challenge the religious aspect that was mentally instilled throughout slavery. The nation of Islam would be the first black nationalist organization to attack the religious aspects of blacks. The nation came about in 1934, however they didn't begin to gain many followers until Malcolm's era. Malcolm X was a prominent black nationalist leader who served as a spokesman for the Nation of Islam during the 1950s and '60s. Due largely to his efforts, the Nation of Islam grew from a mere 400 members at the time he was released from prison in 1952 to 40,000 members by 1960. Articulate, passionate and a naturally gifted and inspirational orator, Malcolm X exhorted blacks to cast off the shackles of racism "by any means necessary," including violence. Malcolm X, the activist and outspoken public voice of the Black Muslim faith, challenged the mainstream civil rights movement and the nonviolent pursuit of integration championed by Martin Luther King Jr. He urged followers to defend themselves against white aggression "by any means necessary." Charismatic and eloquent, Malcolm became an influential leader of the Nation of Islam, which combined Islam with black nationalism and sought to encourage and disenfranchise disadvantaged young blacks searching for confidence in segregated America. After Malcolm X's death in 1965, his bestselling book The Autobiography of Malcolm X popularized his ideas, particularly among black youth, and laid the foundation for the Black Power movement of the late 1960s and 1970s. (http://www.history. com/ topics/black-history/malcolm-x2009) of all of prominent leaders none had ever challenged the religious belief, and nor would it affect the conscious development of blacks. Dubois and Booker T Washington debate was not as emotionally charged as Malcolm and Martin. Nor did Dubois or Washington promote violence or a hate attitude toward America. {Martin approached differed from Malcolm just as his religious perspectives. King came from a comfortable middle class family steeped in the tradition of the Southern black ministry: both his father and maternal grandfather were Baptist preachers. His parents were college-educated, and King's father had succeeded his father-in-law as pastor of the prestigious Ebenezer Baptist Church in Atlanta. The family lived on Auburn Avenue, otherwise known as "Sweet Auburn," Young Martin received a solid education and grew up in a loving extended family. In the years from 1960 to 1965, King's influence reached its zenith. Handsome, eloquent, and doggedly determined, King quickly caught the attention of the news media, particularly of the producers of that budding medium of social change—television. He understood the power of television to nationalize and internationalize the struggle for civil rights, and his well-publicized tactics of active nonviolence (sit-ins, protest marches) aroused the devoted allegiance of many African Americans and liberal whites in all parts of the country, as well as support from the administrations of Presidents Kennedy and Lyndon B. Johnson. But there were also notable failures, as in Albany, Georgia (1961–62), when King and his colleagues failed to achieve their desegregation goals for public parks and other facilities.}

Chapter 22

Part 1 Religion and Indoctrination

True Islam taught me that it takes all of the religious, political, economic, psychological, and racial ingredients, or characteristics, to make the Human Family and the Human Society complete.

<u>**Malcolm X**</u>

African American religious cultures were born in the crucible of American slavery, a system that not only ruptured direct connections to African history, culture, and religious community, but also set the context for the emergence of transformed and new religious systems. As African Americans embraced Christianity in the 18th century, especially after 1770, they gathered in independent church communities and created larger denominational structures such as the African Methodist Episcopal Church, the African Methodist Episcopal Zion Church, and the National Baptist Convention. Black religious institutions served as contexts in which African Americans made meaning of the experience of enslavement, interpreted their relationship to Africa, and charted a vision for a collective future. The Great Migration of southern blacks to southern and northern cities fostered the development of a variety of religious options outside of Christianity. Groups such as the Moorish Science Temple and the Nation of Islam, whose leaders taught that Islam was the true religion of people of African descent, and congregations of Ethiopian Hebrews promoting Judaism as the heritage of black people, were founded in this period. Early-20th-century African American religion was also marked by significant cultural developments as ministers, musicians, actors, and other performers turned to new media, such as radio, records, and film, to contribute to religious life. (Judith Weisenfeld march2015). The black population was totally indoctrinated to the Christian culture that was implemented during slavery. However, due to slave's not feeling equal to the masters and white counterparts only on Sunday, soon became a dream deferred. Blacks looked to obtain freedom through religion once they began to interpret the scripture from their own perspectives. Blacks looked at the scriptures and began to identify how they were used to create a psychological enslavement. Bible verses that was utilize to push the acceptance of slavery was "Ephesians 6:4-6: Fathers, do not exasperate your children; instead, bring them up in the training and instruction of the Lord. Slaves, obey your earthly masters with respect and fear, and with sincerity of heart, just as you would obey Christ. Obey them not only to win their favor when their eye is on you, but like slaves of Christ, doing the will of God from your heart. Ephesians 6:5:Slaves, obey your earthly masters with respect and fear, and with sincerity of heart, just as you would obey Christ. Ephesians 6:9 And masters, treat your slaves in the same way. Do not threaten them, since you know that he who is both their Master and yours is in heaven, and there is no favoritism with him. Colossians 3:22:Slaves, obey your earthly masters in everything; and do it, not only when their eye is on you and to win their favor, but with sincerity of heart and reverence for the Lord. Colossians 4:1:Masters, provide your slaves with what is right and fair, because you know that you also have a Master in heaven. Titus 2:9:Teach slaves to be subject to their masters in everything, to try to please them, not to talk back to them,1 Peter 2:18:Slaves, submit yourselves to your masters with all respect, not only to those who are good and considerate, but also to those who are harsh. Slave owners would read these verses to slaves as part of the worship services that they allowed (and controlled) as a means of encouraging the proper attitude among their slaves. Based upon these isolated verses, slave owners claimed that the Bible supported slavery and taught slaves to be obedient to their masters. Slave's began to branch away from the Christianity that was taught by the salve owners, they now interpreted from their own perspective. With roots from history in the wind, blacks moved into the 20th century with their religious belief. The belief in god was expressed through art and literature and depicted from a black perspective. Up until the 1930's there were no influential factors that challenged the religious standpoint of blacks. With the birth of black national groups discussed above, none would have an influence to change the religious context of the masses of blacks. Religion was the head front of black household, they attached all their success and freedom to their answered prayers." In the ante-bellum South where slavery was king, the theological paradigm was 'Exodus'. The slaves identified with the children of Israel in Egyptian bondage and saw the hand of God at work in terms of their hope in deliverance from slavery. This theology addressed the issues of survival, refuge and resistance to oppression."(Adam Edgerly and Carl Ellis) Noble drew Ali, and Elijah Muhammad would be the first to change the psychological thinking of blacks, they would utilize religion and documented fact of our origin to dispute the present concept that blacks were indoctrinated with. They provided facts into how blacks were manipulated by the scriptures to psychologically and socially attach to servitude as a norm. with the Moor scientist, and Nation of Islam establishing temples, and mosques within the U.S., they still were not able to reach the majority of the black Americans, leaving their ranks to a small amount of followers. Even though their rhetoric was promoting black nationalist attitudes, and the total abolishment of Christianity, neither group was able to gain the vast majority. There are a number of factors into why they were unable to reach the masses, maybe because television and media wasn't as effective as in the 50's. with the emergence of Malcolm X, gave the nation the notoriety it had so long expected. swelling their membership to 40,000, Malcolm X proved to be the natural born leader the nation so long desired. under Elijah, the nation's numbers were at a standstill. Malcolm was able to get the message the nation was striving to get out to the masses for 18 years before Malcolm. As television came full surface, Malcolm was able to gain media attention as he attacked civil rights leaders and their religious views. This brought the split between Islam and Christianity. Islam had no place in America until Malcolm X gave it the notoriety. There is history of Islam in America dating back to the first slave captors that were brought to America, a small percentage were Muslim. "A small but significant proportion of African slaves, some estimate 10 percent, were Muslim. You might tell the story of Omar Ibn Said (also "Sayyid," ca. 1770-1864), who was born in Western Africa in the Muslim state of Futa Toro (on the south bank of the Senegal River in present-day Senegal). He was a Muslim scholar and trader who, for reasons historians have not uncovered, found himself captive and enslaved. After a six-week voyage, Omar arrived in Charleston, South Carolina, in about 1807. About four years later, he was sold to James Owen of North Carolina's Cape Fear region."(Thomas A. Tweed). African Muslims were present during the first generation of slaves that were transported to the America's. (, but converts have been more prominent among Americans of African descent, especially those who followed the mass migrations of southern blacks to northern cities beginning in the early decades of the twentieth century. Noble Drew Ali established a Black nationalist Islamic community, the Moorish Science Temple, in Newark, New Jersey in 1913. After his death in 1929, one of the movement's factions found itself drawn to the mysterious Wallace D. Fard, who appeared in Detroit in 1930 preaching black nationalism and Islamic faith. Fard founded the Nation of Islam there in the same year. After Fard's unexplained disappearance in 1934, Elijah Muhammed (1897-1975) took over, and he attracted disenchanted and poor African Americans from the urban north. They converted for a variety of reasons, but, for some, the poverty and racism in those cities made the Nation of Islam's message about "white devils" (and "black superiority") plausible.) The information that the nation of islam represented had mirrored that of the Sunni. The nation considered Elijah Muhammad as the last prophet, and that W.D. Fard was Allah in person. By adhering to the disenchanted and poor blacks within the urban north, the nation depicted white America to the inner city in the most gruesome form. The imagery and social injustice that blacks were subjected to during these times, made it easy to have psychological attachment to this imagery and be influenced by the information especially with most blacks suffering from P.T.S.D. by way of white America.. Blacks were suffering from post-traumatic stress, depression, and oppression all at the same time. These conditions would lead one to find a way to rid themselves of the social psycho condition that developed their social cognition. The despair that blacks felt while confined to the mental incarceration of their social condition, resulted into the above mental conditions. This can be the reason why a high percentage of black male have an anti personality disorder. The social condition of most black's situation reflected in their eyes the social injustice done by white America. This was embedded in the minds of most black's, furthermore causing them to psychological lock into this theory. as the 50's roared in Islam still did not have a significant hold on African American's. The Christian influence was still heavy within the households where two parents were present. In the 50's black two parent family structures were between 80-76%. Unfortunately, the generation that would be born in the late 30's would change the perspective on the black consciousness, and also denounce their Christian upbringing. The Christian influence was heavy in the south, and with black migrating from the south to the north and west, those Christian values stayed with most. The generation that followed and was born in the late 30's and 40's would soon get the voice it needed to influence their consciousness in a radical way. The new generation was through with M.L.K. non violent protest in which blacks watched from television as other blacks were beaten, killed, hosed, and bitten by dogs. Most were emotionally attached to what they saw, which made them miss the outcome of M.L.K. views. Blacks attached to the violence that was being inflicted, and mental imagery of turning the other cheek. Turning the other cheek wasn't seen by black's from an intellectual perspective, but by an emotional perspective that was attached to the theory as a form of cowardice. Failure to see the dynamics of nonviolent civil disobedience, resulted in angry youth emotionally charged with a hatred that was growing from the oppression endured from the white race. The 50's would be the clash of conditions that would send black family structure pummeling. As rumors of integration began to seep, white's became more hostile, and their attitude towards blacks had increased. The west coast was now witnessing the brutality of the L.A.P.D., which consisted of southern whites that would migrate west to California. A percentage of the southern whites that migrated was part of the K.K.K. Some of the members became members of the L.A.P.D., furthermore implementing the same hatred that fueled the klan to now be present within law enforcement. Police brutality increased in the 50's, with segregation still present, blacks were subjected to demoralization of character, social injustice and social inequality. The prayers of blacks were still going

unanswered, and the youth taking a different approach This would psychologically make

sense, the new generation of blacks looked at their conditions, and the fact that they

supposedly believed in the same god as white did but questioned their conditioning. As

integration began to become more of a fact, whites became hostile, and the new generation

of blacks would begin to see the undeniable racism that America was built on. Youth as

young as 14 would have some form of prejudice or racism inflicted upon them. Looking at

self-imagery and environmental factors at this time, Blacks were forced into the worst of

conditions, and everywhere they turned signs read, "colored only, or white only." To

consistently see these signs, and know that where the sign said "whites only", consisted of

the best of the best, and where the sign read colored only, consisted of the worst of the

worst. This particular daily image matched with constant racial slurs, and discrimination,

one would soon begin to question a religious belief that is shared between white and black.

Faith would only hold so long while the baton constantly strikes you reminding you that you

are not yet free. As the hostility tripled, so did the roar of the lion. Malcolm X would stand

firm as the representative for black America. Black America would embrace Malcolm

because they felt as though they could trust him. Malcolm's words caused a ripple effect

within the black communities." (I am a Muslim, because it's a religion that teaches you an

eye for an eye and a tooth for a tooth. It teaches you to respect everybody, and treat

everybody right. But it also teaches you if someone steps on your toe, chop off their foot.

And I carry my religious ax with me all the time.3) **Malcolm X**

The greatest miracle Christianity has achieved in America is that the black man in white

Christian hands has not grown violent. It is a miracle that 22 million black people have

not risen up against their oppressors – in which they would have been justified by all

moral criteria, and even by the democratic tradition! It is a miracle that a nation of black

people has so fervently continued to believe in a turn-the-other-cheek and heaven-for-you-

after-you-die philosophy! It is a miracle that the American black people have remained a peaceful people, while catching all the centuries of hell that they have caught, here in white man's heaven! The miracle is that the white man's puppet Negro 'leaders', his preachers and the educated Negroes laden with degrees, and others who have been allowed to wax fat off their black poor brothers, have been able to hold the black masses quiet until now."— Malcolm X, The Autobiography of Malcolm X

Quotes such as the above would be what the negro population needed added with their already social conditions and social injustice. Blacks embraced this rhetoric all while emotionally attaching to conditions that were being applied by white America. Malcolm's voice spoke courage into the black population. For the first time blacks felt the need to stand up and fight. With images of slavery and lynching, and now with police brutality, blacks were psychological compelled to Malcolm words. As he blatantly spoke derogatory toward Christianity and the white race, angry blacks began to abolish old thinking, and now develop new thinking. The youth attached to this new thinking, and the more they researched into their origin and background, the more they began to remove themselves from Christian morals. In total Malcolm gained over 40,000 followers at this time in the nation of Islam. Malcolm also gained a large amount of followers that didn't join the nation of Islam. The followers that didn't join the nation would take Malcolm's word and create their own political movements to assist in the conditions of blacks. This movement would be the black power movement, the black power movement consisted of black born between 1930-1959, this would be the era that would form the radical vanguard of black America, which would only do our people a disservice. Most members of the black power era had denounced their Christian ties, and took on new belief systems. This would cause a split between the younger and older generation that used the bible, and relied on faith to substantiate their place. The new generation went against the bible, causing issues within the home which were predominantly Christian. the nation of islam seen it fit to destroy the Christian image considering it a tool of white America to keep blacks mentally enslaved. However, during slavery, blacks would soon denounce from the ways they were taught, they began to form there own congregation. They were the A.M.E, A.M.E. Zion, and a host of others. Even though it was used as a ploy to control the masses and manipulate the slave through scriptures, blacks found peace and tranquility within their own interpretation of the scriptures. Their belief would help keep the family setting strong. During the early 1900's, blacks showed growth in economics and industrial work. With conditions as they were, and segregation, blacks were still able to flourish within society. An example of this is black wall street. "The date was June 1, 1921, when "Black Wall Street," the name fittingly given to one of the most affluent all-Black communities in America, was bombed from the air and burned to the ground by mobs of envious whites. In a period spanning fewer than 12 hours, a once thriving 36-Black business district in northern Tulsa lay smoldering--a model community destroyed, and a major African-American economic movement resoundingly defused. The night's carnage left some 3,000 African Americans dead, and over 600 successful businesses lost. Among these were 21 churches, 21 restaurants, 30 grocery stores and two movie theaters, plus a hospital, a bank, a post office, libraries, schools, law offices, a half dozen private airplanes and even a bus system. As could have been expected, the impetus behind it all was the infamous Ku Klux Klan, working in consort with ranking city officials, and many other sympathizers." This was evidence of the importance of family structure. Soon after, a new development within black culture was formulating, "The Harlem Renaissance was the name given to the cultural, social, and artistic explosion that took place in Harlem between the end of World War I and the middle of the 1930s. During this period Harlem was a cultural center, drawing black writers, artists, musicians, photographers, poets, and scholars." This era had showcased black's talent in many facets of life. The exposure that came through the Harlem renaissance era gave blacks an enlightenment into identifying their self-worth. The beauty of this cannot be seen by the naked eye, only the intellectually inclined. Not even thirty years out of slavery and blacks were flourishing at a unsurmountable rate. Looking at the businesses that were obtained in the short amount of time displayed the enthuse behind blacks' plight to obtain success. The important factor to keep prevalent is that currently, black two parent family structures were at 90%. This success that black was obtaining at this fast rate, while subject to discrimination, K.K.K., and racism at a all-time high. Also take note that blacks couldn't read and write, but by the 1930, black American had obtained prestigious degrees from some of the country's finest schools. Education and economic growth were the focus in the black homes. They relied on the prayers and hard work. Take note, there were no other influential social elements to conflict with black consciousness. All blacks were based in a Christian belief, and no such thing of black on black crime present.. The black dollar at these times stayed within the black communities. One should be asking themselves, why, why while subjected to lynching, K.K.K., and every form of emotional, physical, and psychological abuse known to man, the blacks at this time possessed a oneness, there was unity, and honor amongst one another. What kept these factors substantial? Two things we can gather is the fact that two parent homes were at 90%, and there were no other religious or social influences. Blacks all had one belief, and that was in the god of their understanding, which they all shared and embraced equally. This is prevalent within immigrants that migrate to the states, no matter the conditioning, the family structure is maintained, and they are embraced by fellow members of their ethnic background. Most immigrants that migrate from the same tribe or culture maintain that belief, and embrace all equally in business and education. When we look at blacks in America, there are too many cultural influences. Unlike other ethic groups, the culture representation is the same based on background or cultural origin. A simple example: a Dominican family of 12 would all have the same cultural and religious perspective during the developmental stages which is between 0-12, after the teen years in some homes the perspectives of some would change based on social and environmental influence. What that means is hypothetical speaking, in a poverty stricken environment that the criminal element is substantial, it's a possibility that 1 to 2 members of the twelve member home will be subject to the environmental factors, but a large majority wont. In black homes, the religious and cultural perspectives are based of ideologies of present black figures, unlike other cultures, the cultural perspective dates back 100's of years prior to. The cultures before the present have lived out the cultural perspective and the effective element that keeps the culture strong remains. This is why when we see immigrants from Africa, and the caribbeans come over, whether they are Nigerian, or from kenya, the Nigerian share cultural perspective as a whole, just as the people from kenya, and so forth. That shared cultural, or religious perspective is what keeps the nation of an ethic group strong. Sure, there will be situations implemented to change the perspective, we have seen this in countries that go to war. In America, the black race has not been able to attach to a cultural perspective, most have either taking a religious perspective geared toward Christianity, Islam, and a slew of other grass root cultural that formulated based off the social conditioning. What this displays is that most black organizations are formulated off emotion, and this is why some lack a political and economically sound plan. This was seen within the black panthers, 5%, B.L.A., bloods, crips, etc. the above mention were all formed of a emotional response to the social condition they were subjected to, what this represent is that where there is heavy emotion, the possibility of irrational judgment is high. Is it possible that the demise of these groups so quickly happened because they were formed off emotion, and not intellect? The social influence in black communities has played a significant role in the demise of it. Emotionally charged organizations began to take the forefront following the black power movement.

When striving to identify the social climate that changed the dynamic of the household, A key factor that I will constantly reiterate is that in 1925 black family structures were 85% two parent, up until 1960. It was 72%, which dropped 13% Within the time frame of 1960-64. The two-parent structure went up to 76%, increasing 4% in 4 years. The next statistic is the detriment of the black social condition that eventually led to the decline of the black household. From 1965-1991, black two parent structures went from 76% to in 1991, a negative 67%, which means that 67% of black families were headed by a single parent, and

54% were teenage pregnancies. This took place between 1965-1991. Within this 26 year span, blacks began to receive more privilege's, and more opportunity for advancement. However, as things appear to be getting better on paper, socially they are becoming worse. Why? We now understand that blacks that were relevant in the early 1900's were subjected to harsh times, and there were no laws that protected blacks, however, they still advanced and developed the majority of our historical figures. Now activists from the 60's and beyond took a more radical approach, which was the opposite of our past activists. From 1960-1972, we watch a slew of subcultures transgress, Bloods, Crips, Gangsta Disciples, vice lords, latin kings, 5%, p-stone rangers, sons of Malcolm X, B.L.A., M.O.V.E.,etc. Each of these sub-groups fashioned their ideology of the black panthers. The Panthers formulated their concept of Malcolm X theory and perspectives, not El-Hajj El Malik.

"It is also clear that Malcolm X had a strong influence on the individual, personal philosophies of key Black Panther members, especially the two founding members. Both Huey P. Newton and Bobby Seale were drawn in by Malcolm's speeches and agreed with many of the revolutionary ideas he expressed within them. Bobby Seale wrote about listening to Malcolm X's speeches, proclaiming him to be "a better speaker than even Martin Luther King." He went on to name his son Malik Nkrumah Stagolee Seale, later explaining "Malik" was "for Malcolm X". After Malcolm's death, Seale wrote that he "cried like a baby" and announced soon afterwards: "I will make my own self into a motherf**king Malcolm X...they'll have to kill me!" In the process, Seale made clear the extent to which Malcolm X had influenced his belief."

"Huey Newton's personal philosophies were similarly influenced by Malcolm X in the years prior to the formation of the Black Panther Party. Newton claimed that Malcolm's work with the Organization of Afro-American Unity was one of the major sources of inspiration in him eventually forming the Black Panther Party and gave him enormous credit in paving the way for the party's eventual rise. Newton was sure that despite leaders like Martin Luther King advocating non-violence in the struggle for civil rights, Malcolm

X, with his policy of armed self-defence, had the only philosophy which could bring real success in the struggle against white oppression. Newton wrote that he saw the Black Panther Party as "a living testament to [Malcom X's] life work" and Newton was especially influenced by Malcolm's desire to help educate black people and encourage a sense of black pride and an appreciation of their heritage."

Bobby Seale words establishes my theory of how most black organization were designed based of an emotional attachment to the situation at hand. The black panther party gave way to the sub-cultures, which most came into play between 1969-1975, when the B.P.P. was beginning to dismantle. Is it possible as the B.B.P. began to dismantle members choose to leave and join, or possibly create their own subculture? The possibilities vary. What is becoming evident is that something occurred, the question is what. Statistic tells us that between 1965-1991, the incarceration, and crime rate had seen a vast increase. Black community faced destructive times from the 60's on. Looking at the dynamics of how a social setting can affect the total population, we must analyze the time in retrospect to gain insight into what administered the decline. As we know, the inner doing within the home in black inner cities will eventually sprawl out into the community and create a social norm. influential social factors are the initial steps toward the infiltration into the social cognition of blacks. To attack social cognition, one must have utilized empathetic measures that adhere to the conscious sciences of the said person. Looking at what black's issues lied within, most would determine the empathetic measures used to conform the mentality, would focus primarily on the concern of the group. Those concerns were wrapped around issues that blacks felt whites were the reason behind, the dreams deferred. This social perspective along with the gruesome pictures and images of slavery, along with the violent murders of innocent black children, the four girls and emit till. These death hit black communities hard across the country, with emit till death in 1955, august 28, the murder of 4 black girls September 1963, then right before that, the brutal murder of Medgar Evers, and 1965 El-Hajj El Malik Shabazz. The country would face a social dilemma in

1955, once the brown vs board case came into play, banning segregation of schools. This was the start of the social climate, with integration, and the death of blacks mentioned above. It was unethical, and it was becoming an emotional and psychological strain on most blacks. This strain mixed with financial issues, and inadequate housing, black as a whole began to subject to a depressed state of mind. The outlook was hopelessness, as we watched the country move from slavery to Jim crow, to now actual ridding the world of Jim Crow, only to be placed in the same condition's blacks were subjected to during slavery, and Jim Crow. One can only feel a sense of despair, to actually understand the context of black history, and to see laws and moral codes change, only to still be identified as not equal would affect the psychological processing of anyone. As the above issues were formulating within black communities all over the world, Malcolm words were falling upon the ears of the black community. His blatant discrimination and derogatory attitude towards whites made blacks feel a sense of hope when Malcolm emerged. Blacks were now looking for a new leader, they watched Martin and the plight to change the laws, which did happen, however the racial prejudice was embedded in the souls of some white folks so no matter what laws were changed, they would never socially accept blacks as their equal. The population watched the turn of events that occurred between 1955-1965, Malcolm word would take a social influence causing 40,000 plus blacks to denounce their Christian origin and embrace the N.O.I. Not to mention, there was a large percentage of black that took Malcolm perspectives, but didn't join the Nation. However, they too would soon denounce their Christian upbringing. This would bring about a social dilemma within the black communities. The large percentage that developed Malcolm perspectives but chose to personalize them, would formulate the new vanguard of the black population, bringing in the black power movement. With this split within religion, this affected the household of blacks. A visual understanding of this is seen in the movie "The Butler ". the split would be The children attaching Malcolm vision, and the adults maintaining their Christian origin which were more geared toward Dr. King views. Tempers would be introduced as constant debates between the new conscious, versus the old conscious. This split would be one way of breaking down the effect of what was to come. Looking at history, this would be the first social influence that attacked the religious components that blacks attached to. As the condition and racism worsened, the more the mental perception of the new generation changed and took a radical approach that was emotionally fueled. Analyzing this time period, we can identify key components that involve cognitive development within the black community. The Nation of Islam had a dynamic effect on the cultural perspective of black America, and without Malcolm X gaining the media exposure, and the confidence of the people, his word would change the social climate that would change the perspective of how blacks were now looking at the world.. By adopting this method, it would soon place black in a position where their accountability would lessen, and their issues would always result in the white man. By taking this bias approach, one could utilize this as to justify his or her wrong doing. Reason being, Malcolm's words, if listened to closely, never told blacks about what they could do to better the situation, it was always what the white man should do. As blacks became psychologically inclined to place the blame on their entire situation on whites, eventually caused blacks to live in denial and become non-receptive to accountability. Malcolm's words caused his followers to take the victim stance on all facets of their life, even when their actions were the results of their consequences. This became a crutch, and many blacks used whites as a scapegoat for what they were not doing collectively. .

Chapter 23

"Everybody can be great, because anybody can serve. You don't have to have a college degree to serve. You don't have to make your subject and verb agree to serve... You only need a heart full of grace. A soul generated by love

Martin Luther King Jr

The eagerness to succeed was evident, the mentality was all the same and the social influence was all the same as well as the religious perspective.

When we understand the concept of social influence and the part it plays in our everyday life, only then will one be able to identify with the part in which they play in the destruction of self-identity. Looking within the text, we have been able to identify with social psychology that aids in the cognition of the black race, or any ethic group. As blacks face barriers to developing a successful life while dealing with social injustice, and social inequality, it's important to understand the part in which you aid. The inferiority, and insecurity that exist within a person's cognition, and maladaptive schemas are what molds a person social perspective. maladaptive schema is defined as broad, pervasive themes regarding one's self, and one's relationship with others, developed during childhood and elaborated. Maladaptive schema's are developed during the preoperational stage of development, these schema's consist of; abandonment, instability, mis-trust, abuse, defectiveness, shame, social isolation, alienation, dependence, incompetence, failure to achieve, etc. one of the most important maladaptive schema that plagues the inner city is, emotional deprivation, Expectation that one's desire for a normal degree of emotional support will not be adequately met by others. The three major forms of deprivation are:A. Deprivation of Nurturance: Absence of attention, affection, warmth, or companionship. B. Deprivation of Empathy: Absence of understanding, listening, self-disclosure, or mutual sharing of feelings from others. C. Deprivation of Protection: Absence of strength, direction, or guidance from others. Looking at emotional deprivation, which is number 3 under the maladaptive schemas, this I define as the bass root to gaining insight into the family condition. Emotional deprivation is broken down in three perspectives, lack of nurturance, empathy, and protection. Emotional deprivation became vital within the black communities as the 70's rolled in. mass incarceration was in effect, Data throughout crime statistics revealed the following. The data that is shown reflect from the year 1970 and 1979. Crimes of violence went from 738,820-1,208,030, property crime 7,359,200-11,041,500, murder 16,000-21,460, rape 37,990-76,390, robbery 349,860-480,700, assault 334,970-629,480, burglary 2,205,000-3,327,700, and vehicle theft 928,400-1,112,800. With the increase of crime, black made up a large percentage of incarcerated males for the above crimes. During the 70's with the riots sprawling out, crime began to invade the inner cities as a means of survival, and initial survival moves started to become the norm. Most will succumb to the life of crime based on emotional deprivation. The emotional deprivation that came from the homes due to single parenting, will cause a person to search out for the things they were deprived of. A recent study was performed to identify with children that didn't receive an emotional attachment to their parents. "While all types of abused children are likely to have low self-esteem, poor ego control, (they are inflexible or impulsive) process negative feelings about themselves and their environment. Those who are physically abused tend to show more anger and frustration and to be more hyperactive, whereas those reared by psychologically unavailable mothers tend to be more withdrawn and highly dependent and to suffer the most severe decline in mental and behavioral development as they get older." Emotional deprivation leads to feelings of abandonment and instability, this particular maladaptive schema is perceived as instability or unreliability of those available for support or connection. These feelings can come by way of so many years of emotional deprivation, one can develop the outlook as if no one is there for them, and not aware of what it feels to be loved. This causes children to internalize social conditions that they have yet grown to understand. Feeling of abandonment will lead to feelings of mistrust when dealing with people that can be genuinely sincere. Emotional deprivation is classified as a form of psychological abuse. This abuse leads to underdeveloped children that will have social and psychological hindrances that will prosper into adulthood. "The findings to date are painting a broad new picture of child abuse, challenging many long-held beliefs about its causes and consequences, and its very nature. For example, the study has shown that poverty and inordinate life stress alone do not cause child abuse and that the nature and effects of abuse go far beyond beatings, bruises and broken bones. About half the abused children in the study would never be identified as in need of help by child protection agencies because they do not fit the classical definition of life-threatening physical abuse or neglect." Looking at the black population, these findings can lead us to see that poverty is not the overall issue, nor the social inequality and injustice of white America, does not have the effect on the black population as does its own internal destruction. which is the individualistic perspective that has replaced the collectivist perspective. As the 70's came in black population home fronts began to rise in poverty, but worst of all emotional deprivation. The nurturance that was present prior to the 60's is what made that a particular generation flourished, that's evident just knowing that in 1925 black families were at 85% dual parent homes, with the only influence being religion. That religion was the belief in one god. Blacks were joined by love, religion, and prosperity. From the 60's and beyond, the dynamic changed, and this change came by way of consciousness and social inequality and injustice. As the consciousness took a turn, so did the black family infrastructure, the black power rhetoric was in full swing, and the new generation were beginning to part ways from the old. The new generation would soon rebel against the generation of the old and the birth of subcultures and black nationalist groups began to sprawl up all over the country. The birth of black nationalist groups, and sub-cultures also defined as gangs, was the emotional rebellion of blacks toward the systematic social system that was causing poverty, and depression. Social blacks were depressed and were seeking an advancement out of the depression. The conditioning was severe, and the psychological outlook to most was deferred due to racism. The depression quickly rose to a head, and exploded. That conscious explosion that was fathered by Malcolm X, and the Nation of Islam, mixed with police brutality, and a slew of other factors, caused blacks to internalize psychological stressors, then externalize which was the birth of rioting. The riots, and the new consciousness showed how black America has been emotionally deprived from its mother country. By not possessing the connection needed to thrive in life, the emotional deprivation from not having an identification to attach to a culture of their own was welcomed in the phenomenon of social influence, which then transferred to media influence. The power of social influence by way of emotional attachment to the situation, but underdeveloped to fully understand the situation, will cause dysfunction within the social cognition, which will then produce a psychological outlook later developing an environmental factor, which then will birth the social conditioning. The emotional deprivation blacks received as a whole, along with impoverished conditions, eventually began to invade the home front. Prior to the 60's this invasion was unable to invade the homes, at a time when the conditions and opportunities for success were vague, in comparison to present. This gives substance to my hypothesis on the transformation and the cause behind it. In the 1890s, there were four public high schools in Washington D.C.; one black, the M Street School/Dunbar High School, and three white. In 1899, Dunbar averaged higher standardized test scores than students in two of the three white schools. From 1870 to 1955 Dunbar repeatedly equaled or exceeded performance on national standardized tests. As late as 1910 more than two-thirds of the black population of Chicago lived in neighborhoods where most residents were white. In 1925 85% of black families were 2 parents. In 1950, 72 percent of all black men and 81 percent of black women had been married. Every census from 1890 to 1950 showed that black labor force participation rates were higher than those of whites. Prior to the 1960's the unemployment rate for black 16 and 17-year old was under 10 percent. Before 1960, the number of teenage pregnancies had been decreasing; both poverty and dependency were declining, and black income was rising in both absolute and relative terms to white income. In 1965, 76.4 percent of black children were born to married women." Analyzing the statistical fact presented, the evidence is clear, black acceleration in education was beginning to flourish, look at how Dunbar high advanced on a national level, at a time when black racism and discrimination was at an all-time high.. This displayed the unified outlook of the race, there ambition to survive and thrive economically was charged by the mental and physical constraints that were implemented by way of slavery. The eagerness to succeed was evident, the mentality was all the same and the social influence was all the same as well as the religious perspective. Between 1910-1950, black two parent family structure dropped from 85% in 1925 to 72% in 1950, there was a 13% drop, which can be possible due to the war. In 1941 fewer than 4,000 African Americans were serving in the military and by 1945, more than 1.2 million African Americans would be serving in uniform. This could possibly contribute to the 13% decline. At this time, the social influence that was prevalent after slavery would still be present in 1950. Many of the deaths of soldiers during world war 2 and the Korean war would affect the family structure of both black and white. However, white family structure declining, unfortunately poverty, and racism would not affect whites. Also note that, black nationalist movements that challenged the religious component still didn't have an effect on black population as a whole. At this time the Nation of Islam only had only several mosque, so their influence was not as influential as when Malcom entered the ranks in 1952. Within the stats we are able to see that the incline of black success and education when families promoted education. This is evident just by looking at black wall street and the Harlem renaissance era, this would define the power of black intellect unified for one cause which was to rise as a nation equally amongst themselves, and to serve god until atonement. This was black's perspective, this was their self-identification into identifying with who they are as a people. They wanted equal success and depriving your own was unheard of. This evidence is displayed in the birth of great women and men that came out of this era. Unfortunately after 1959, things would take a turn. To identify this turn within the group, the information presented in prior chapters show the dynamical change in the race as a group constituted 78% of shooting suspects and 74% of all shooting victims even though they are less than 23% of the city's population. Young black men in New York are 36 times more likely to be murdered than young white men. Today, black males between the ages of 14 and 17 commit homicide at ten times the rate of white and Hispanic males of the same age combined. In many urban areas, the black illegitimacy rate is well over 80 percent. The national unemployment rate for blacks is over 13%, nearly five points above the average for all Americans. And black teen unemployment is over 40 %." (Dean Kalahar 2014)

Chapter 24

Social movement

Factoring the above information, we can revert to the information within the text to identify with what concurred to cause the black family infrastructure to pummel. Statistical facts presented determine that within the black community something occurred to subject the black community into an impediment of this magnitude. From 1965 on, we watched the black family decline at a rate far more imaginable than actual, but a mere fact. The perplexity of this matter showed how social influence became the problem, along with the multiple cultural development over a 80 year span. The black mind and conscious is made up of, Christian, Pan-Africanism, Moorish scientist, N.O.I., BBP, Blood, Crip, isrealities, 5%, Muslim, BLA, M.OV.E., and a host of others. Black Americans may be the only culture of people that has this many cultural influences within a short span of time. Looking deeper into the above cultures within the black communities, all are the direct response to the racism and social injustice within society. Each was made or indoctrinated by white principles or to combat white principles toward blacks. Most of the above cultures had its biggest influence from the 60's and beyond. From 1959 and before, the only cultural influence that controlled the masses of black consciousness was the religion of Christianity. The NOI and the moors were present, but they had little cultural influence currently. The nation began to gain its followers once Malcolm took center stage. After the nation came most of the other cultural influences except pan Africanism. The birth of these cultural influences sent the black community into a frenzy. Malcolm's death would mark the beginning of the end, with the Watts riot kicking off months after his death, his words were echoed as rioters looted and damaged property, all behind the ideology of Malcolm X, not El Hajj-El Malik Shabazz. At the brink of the riots formed the BBP this would be the second biggest influential movement within black history. The panther's fashion their rhetoric of off Malcolm X's nation of Islam ideology and created a movement that would gain the attention of the inner city at a magnitude greater then Malcolm. The panthers managed to establish 68 branches in 68 cities in the US, and a branch in Algiers. What was remarkable about this movement and what made their influence greater than Malcolm's, was that the panthers managed to establish multiple branches, food programs, health clinics, and so forth within a 4-year process. From 1966, which was the birth year of the panthers, to 1970, which was when the panthers started to see a decline, and also the rank went from Huey P Newton, to Elaine Brown, this was possible done to give the panthers a new imagine with a feministic touch, and removing the old radical behavior that they were able to see was not the most intellectual component into reconstructing, and repairing the black race. As the panthers began to diminish, new influences were set to take the stage out west, replacing what was once policed by panthers, were now be patrolled and loitered by bloods and crips. The information at present can assist in understanding the importance of social influence and how it infiltrated black consciousness and created a quandary socially. The generation to come would have the above influences to develop their social cognition all while being emotionally deprived in the home front, exposed to gangs and violence on the outside, and plagued by social injustice and racism. With respect to territorial boundaries, black youth during the 80's began to initiate into gangs at a rapid rate. Black on black crime was beginning to take effect, and drugs were about to be unleashed full blast. The 80's would mark the aftermath of the 60's, and the generation to follow will be far removed from the ways of 1959, and before. The Christian homes that were once the pillar in the black community were now plagued with multiple sub-cultures under one roof. An example can be Harlem NY, a home can consist of a single mother and 3 siblings, hypothetically two boys and a girl, all which were born after 1972. The possibility of multiple sub-cultures influencing one is prevalent. Example, more than likely the mother would be Christian, or possible Muslim due to Malcolm influence in Harlem. More than likely, during the adolescent years of the two boys, the 5% nation of gods and earth was flourishing, and so was the nation. The possibility of one of the boys being Muslim, and the other 5% are strongly possible. Just as In the 2000's there was a strong connection between bloods,

Crips, and Muslims. Within the New Jersey prison system this is common amongst gang affiliates. Some are either blood and Muslim, or Crip and Muslim. The social effect of the sub-cultures brings about the element of organized crime within urban areas, mixed with drugs, which eventually led to black on black crime. As we analyze the information before us, it is evident that blacks conform to social influence as a form of guidance due to circumstantial injustice. And as the homes separated, single parented, and emotionally deprived black youth searched within the environment to gain an identity to grow with. This identity would develop antisocial behavior, and set the stage for mass incarceration to unfold. The environment would eventually be the youth's outlet, which will eventually develop a negative and pessimistic attitude toward anything positive.

Chapter 25

The first point was we wanted power to determine our own destiny in our own black community. And what we had done is, we wanted to write a program that was straightforward to the people. We didn't want to give a long dissertation.

Bobby Seale

Negativity, pessimism, A pervasive, lifelong focus on the negative aspects of life (pain, death, loss, disappointment, conflict, guilt, resentment, unsolved problems, potential mistakes, betrayal, things that could go wrong, etc.) while minimizing or neglecting the positive or optimistic aspects. Usually includes an exaggerated expectation-- in a wide range of work, financial, or interpersonal situations -- that things will eventually go seriously wrong, or that aspects of one's life that seem to be going well will ultimately fall apart. Life involves an inordinate fear of making mistakes that might lead to: financial collapse, loss, humiliation, or being trapped in a bad situation. Because potential negative outcomes are exaggerated, these patients are frequently characterized by chronic worry, vigilance, complaining, or indecision. Analyzing the maladaptive schema of negativity and pessimism. This adheres to the black race of people from a psychological standpoint. That psychological standpoint is wrapped around a sub-conscious of deferred dreams, black look at the negative aspect of life based on their social situation and mental processing. This is huge within the community, due to media depiction of blacks, it gives the world a negative perspective on the people. This perspective gives a demoralizing social perspective. This social perspective creates an illusion to the world that blacks are lazy and worthless. This was internalized within the soul of black folks, furthermore, transferring from generation to generation and becoming part of the psychological destruction of the black image. However, this is an element that has existed since the beginning of time. This distortion of the image of blacks came by way of psychological classification of the black race, interpreted to white America, who eventually attached to the psychological perspective delivered by psychologists, furthermore, acting out in the way socially blacks have been classified. This negative and pessimistic attitude that exists within the black the community

came by way of psychological outlooks that governed the population with racist and

demoralization evidence that was not factual but interpreted as if it was. In the 1920's, Carl

Jung, psychologist stated that, "that the negro has a whole historical layer less in brain,

Jung considered himself a specialist in primitive people, in speculation he proposed that

living within a close proximity. He considered that if blacks began to outnumber whites,

it could cause a serious mental and moral problem. Being classified as primitive already

demoralizes the characteristics of any person, primitive is defined as, a person belonging

to a preliterate, nonindustrial society or culture. Looking at how blacks are defined from

a primitive perspective one can identify how this projection created the concept of white

America toward blacks. Jung identified blacks as not equal to white, based off the primitive

concept that is used to define the black race of people. Primitive is also defined as, relating

to, denoting, or preserving the character of an early stage in the evolutionary or historical

development of something. This coincide with the element of blacks being defined as beast

in which this theory was utilized during slavery, and misrepresented and manipulated to

justify the wrong doing of blacks.

Psychologist Lewis Termin stated, "are uneducated beyond the nearest rudiments of

training. No amount of school instruction will ever make them intelligent voters or capable

citizens in the true sense of the word….their dullness seems to be radical, or at least

inherent from the family stock in which they come…. Children from this group should

be segregated in special classes and be given instruction which is concrete and practical.

They cannot master abstraction, but they can often be made efficient workers…there is no

possibility at present of convincing society that they should be allowed to reproduce."

The psychological classification of blacks from prominent psychologists sub consciously

assisted in programing whites to identify with blacks in this manner. By becoming

part of the subconscious, the behaviors will express that in their demeanor and posture

when dealing with black. By blacks sub-consciously attaching to this psychological interpretation places them at the hands of inferiority. This perspective that blacks were attaching to was not only a psychological inferiority, but also a physical inferiority matched with fear. The misrepresentation of blacks from a psychological point of view has caused whites to feel non-condescending toward blacks and the issues at hand. blacks psychologically interpret the perspective white America has of them, furthermore, placing them in a perspective to feel the need to please. Without a need to please some blacks feel it would jeopardize their success. When your outlook on society has placed you in a mental place where you can only view negative and pessimistic thoughts as your outcome, this is a direct result of the psychological programming that needs to be undone. The overall imagery of black America must be recreated and eliminate the negative imagery that is depicted in our history. This negative imagery of slavery, lynching and the overall mis-treatment of blacks in America give the generations post-traumatic stress, and the historical images of whites and how they demoralized and enslaved blacks, mixed with the social perception of present through media images, would cause one to look at him or herself as less of in comparison to white America. The media depiction of white is advertised with all the things that define success. From constant imagery of blacks in history, along with media depiction of white, it's understandable how a black people can conform to a negative and pessimistic attitude. This is what the environment around creates, and the first step is gaining an identification and a purpose. To continuously accept the purpose and identification that was psychologically imposed will result in a negative and pessimistic attitude toward life, which welcome a variety of psychological conditions that will assist in the destruction of the moral character and place blacks in a state of content with their current situations. This content will result in initial incarceration and recidivism of black males, and our women allowing the system to raise their children. Negative and pessimistic are associated with characteristics that will eventually result in anti-personality disorders. Negative attitude develops a non-condescending attitude which will ignite antisocial behavior. The antisocial personality disorder is prevalent within black males that will eventually face incarceration. The D.S.M. 5 defines anti-personality disorder as the following typical features of anti-personality disorder are failure to conform to lawful and ethical behavior, and an egocentric, callous, lack of concern for others, accompanied by deceitfulness, irresponsibility, manipulative and/or risk taking. Anti-personality disorder is under personality disorders and is defined by characteristics that defy difficulties in identity, self-direction, empathy, and or intimacy, along with specific maladaptive traits. The anti-personality disorder was implemented in 1968, as one of the ten personality disorders. Focusing on how the disorder is defined, it welcomes a negative and pessimistic social perspective, which would cause the development of the disorder. 90% of the inmate population is classified as anti-personality. Looking at the character attributes that define someone displaying the disorder, difficulty in identity, this would be common amongst blacks since blacks struggle with developing an identification due to the removal of cultural and ancestor origin. By blacks lacking this attachment, the sense of self identification has been misplaced, and social influence is the norm. Without an attachment, one can't identify with themselves, or their cultural perspective which was the reason the Christian religion was able to be implemented. Without a direct alliance with a country, black in America were able to be manipulated through the scripture with no alliance, there was no cultural perspective. All people up to present date that come from other countries have an alliance to that country, Muslim that are in the U.S. have an alliance with a country in the middle east, just as china and so forth. Those alliances maintain the culture perspective, and morally the values that are most relevant in that country will follow with them to a new country. With no alliance to a country, blacks' perspective on life became the condition that was forced upon us.

As black identity became striped, they became indoctrinated through white philosophy, and ideology about themselves. Those ideologies created the platform for black consciousness. This consciousness was designated to instill fear, inferiority, and conformity. For hundreds of years this became the mind set of black's during slavery. After so many years, and the depiction of slavery and traumatic event surrounding blacks, the mentality from the slaves remained, as if it is embedded within the soul of black folks. Present day this inferiority still plagues the consciousness of blacks, welcoming the psychological perspective that serves as a detriment to the black race.

Chapter 26

The psychological perspective that affected the developmental progression within most black inner cities, has been socially progressed into a psychological one. What that means is that the social condition creates the psychological condition after a certain amount of time. As those conditions worsen, they begin to affect the social cognition especially if emotion is attached to the conditioning. Emotional attachment to impoverished conditions and all the elements that come with it can lead to depression, anti-personality disorder, anxiety, substance abuse, and alcohol.

After so many years in an impoverished home, and environment, one will develop a negative outlook, that negative outlook would soon transform into anger, which will soon develop a non-caring attitude. This non-caring attitude is the start, and the welcoming of anti-personality disorders. At the welcoming of what psychologists call anti-personality disorder, we would also see the beginning of black on black crime, the re-birth of gang culture and the destruction of the black families. The DSM, which is the diagnostic statistical manual of mental disorders, was first published in 1952. In 1952, the term for anti-personality disorder was like that of antisocial reaction.

Social situations within the black community once the family structure failed, it welcomed a plethora of social conditions. Analyzing the 20th century, we can identify with the change in the family structure. This change sparked a chain of events that would cause black families to become underdeveloped and socially inferior. These social inferiorities result from maladaptive schema, the effect of the maladaptive schemas travel with most throughout adulthood, and are mostly developed within the home. The black family structure is the most important element that needs to be addressed, along with the constant imagery and depiction of blacks that has become part of the younger generation psyche. As black family structure began to fall in 1965, the riots brung a new element that welcomed new social conditions. With the property value decreasing in black communities due the damage that was caused by the riots, black employment rates began to decrease. The property value went down, and soon after the community began to form into ghettos. The street that was once maintained and keep up to par, was now becoming littered with trash and graffiti. Trash that began to invade the street were now the insides of the homes sprawling out and affecting the environment. As subcultures hit, the environment began to face a new dilemma, that was black on black crime. From the years 1965-present, we watch the population of black American stand united with black power, and expressing love and happiness for their people, to hate envy, and the senseless murder of one another. This time frame was watched as blacks that were business owners got an abundance of support from the community, and now black businesses don't receive much support from their own, nor from any other ethnic group. This non-support causes black businesses to fail, and furthermore assist in keeping blacks economically behind. One should question the severe change in such a short amount of time. Looking at the change, one should focus on the era before the change, to fully understand how the change came into effect, then and only would blacks be able to erase the psychological condition. The psychological condition of the said issue welcomes what I call free flowing forms of inferiority. Different forms of inferiority came into play due to media influence. The depiction of white through media interpretation and the social interpretation causes different cultures to take an inferior approach when dealing with whites. When it comes to blacks, the psychological condition that was implemented, and passed down through slavery, welcomed a new forum of condition that blacks would face that would be the final detriment. The final detriment of a culture or race is when the genocide is being done by its own kind. An inferiority complex occurs when the feeling of inferiority is intensified. Symptoms of discouragement or failure can set into the social perception and cause one to see the world from blind eyes. Those blinds eyes become only visible to the environment around them, furthermore, resulting in becoming a product of the said environment whether good or bad. Symptoms of inferiority consist of a multitude of factors ranging from discouragement, insecurities, low self-esteem, and it can also elicit depression the traits could mold character. Inferiority can be implemented in children as young as 4. Black households hold accountability and assist in the development of the child's cognition to accepting inferiorities. Example, if a household constantly speaks about their current conditions, and utilizes white America as the blame, the child will only grow to accept the same. This acceptance lowers the standards, furthermore, developing a socially insecure perspective, that will cause insecurities when dealing with white. This effect came by way as a means of justification for one's conditions once they became in denial about the part they play in the financial and social situation. Analyzing maladaptive schema, I was able to determine which affected the black communities most. emotional deprivation, the schema is broken down in three forms, A. Deprivation of Nurturance:

Absence of attention, affection, warmth, or companionship.

Deprivation of nurturance is vital toward the development of the child. Lack of affection, warmth or companionship as a child causes emotional imbalances. Analyzing the concept of absence of attention is a direct result of the absentee fathers. Focusing on the absentee father, the prevalence of this can be compared to the F.B.I. crime statistics, from 1965-1991 acts of violence went from 387,390 to 1,911,770, murder 9,960-24,700, robbery 138,690-687,730,rape 23,410-106,490, assault 215,330-1,092,740, burglary 1,282,500- 3,157,200,and vehicle theft 496,900- 1,661,700. Prisoners under state and federal jurisdiction went from in 1970 a little 300,00 to 2014, a little over 1,500,000. Information of such can give insight into the demise of the black family structure, with a large percentage of blacks representing a high percent of the incarcerated. The correlation is evident, as the division with the black family structure hit, and subcultures and radical movements were coming into play, the radical element created a violent temperament within blacks, causing a high percent of males to develop anti-personality disorders. These anti-personality disorders gave way to the epidemic of crime that began to transpire within black communities between 1965-1991. Robbery, vehicle theft, and burglary were crime that a large percentage of blacks were arrested for. As the crime rate increased, so did the incarceration rate for black male.

Following the black power movement the criminal element began to sprawl out. Sub-cultures were taking over inner cities streets and corners. Turf wars were conspiring, and just analyzing the spike within the murder rate, we know a large percent consisted of black on black murders. As sub-cultures were gaining heavy recruitment on a daily basis, every square inch of urban terrain became occupied by a particular set, or gang. From 1965-1975, murder went from 9,960-20,510, which consist of 10,000 increase over the ten year span, and doubling the 1965 number. The information is based on the total population, however we can identify with the black population being heavily involved in the country's judicial matters. What is grime about the image that is being painted is, drug offenses are not mentioned as of yet. Analyzing the data presented, we could see how emotional deprivation began to affect the homes. With crime rising, and black fathers becoming involved with the criminal element, incarceration developed into a social norm, and teenage pregnant mothers began to raise the children of the men that were incarcerated. In 1991, 54% of black pregnancies were teenage mothers, and 67% of black children were being raised in single parent homes. This formulated emotional deprivation, with young black single mothers, forced to work two or three jobs, while others stayed home and did nothing. This is when social influence became influential, after M.L.K. death, blacks had no strong activist to confide in and feel compelled to represent. It was as if after Malcolm and Martin, blacks became psychological and sociological lost, and at this point is when the social influence was at a head. With the destruction of strong black leaders becoming nonexempt, the population only felt compelled to follow one person, and that was minister louis Farrakhan. However, the same element would be relevant, black that didn't agree with the nation in the past would still take the same stance as in the past, predominantly based on religious factors. No other black since Malcolm or Martin has had a heavy influence on the consciousness of black like the BBP, and minister Farrakhan whom organized the million-man march and re-established the nation of Islam. Unfortunately, this was the same element that caused the division within black families, and the information was the same when

Malcolm spoke. The nation was the only black organization that maintained an economical, and political plan and lived it out. Farrakhan's ideologies are not agreed by many, however there is no denying his dedication to the betterment of his race. Active activist of the past had faded with the family structure. As the single parenting for blacks increased during the seventies, so did poverty. And when I say poverty, I mentally impoverished, stating that blacks are one of the biggest contributors to the economic system within America. From the seventies to present, the black community didn't feel compelled to join with the new activist like Sharpton, and Jackson as they did Garvey, King, Malcolm, or Huey. The years after the seventies shows the decline in the conscious, and educational development of blacks.

Chapter 27

The generational social conditions that evolved from the 60's developed into harsher living conditions, limited opportunities for employment and the emergence of a new sub-cultural that would surface full blast and establish a reputation across the country. Looking at the 1970's, we watched as civil rights transgressed to the black power movement, to the black power movement transforming into the sub-cultural movement" Small & Newman, 2001; Sullivan, 1989): there was a recession, manufacturing plants moved to the sunbelt and abroad, many of the employers that remained in the North moved to suburban areas placing them out of the range of public-transportation for inner-city residents, and the new economy emphasized advanced education and computer literacy. Many African Americans were left unemployed and unqualified for emerging opportunities" as the 70's went out, there was a new phenomenon taking place, and that was the birth of technology. With technology coming into play which consisted of the computer age, and advanced education, blacks were way behind. With most black migrating to the north for industrial work, most blacks didn't feel education was needed to feed your family, work was now the forefront of the household. Most black men at that time were uneducated, and as the 80's came in with technology, it began displacing blacks at the workplace. Crack would hit the inner cities to make up for the financial loss, but unfortunately it would only add to the social condition that has derived over the past 20 years. The 80's would be defined as the dark era, I state dark era because there were no conscious movements, and most were left searching for an identity, and an understanding of their condition all while battling police brutality. The 80's and beyond would be better years as far as opportunities for blacks, but these years would be defined as the epitome of the black race. This group was the most unconscious, and unintellectual generation of blacks. I say that because there were no strong cultural leaders, nor were there any advocates for the inner-city blacks. The 80's would show the dynamic within the separation of the black race unity. With the Cosby show depicting the new image for blacks, unfortunately there were blacks that were still suffering from the social conditions of the inner city, and the injustice of America. The socioeconomic system that has been implemented is also shown within the black community. Most of the blacks that became educated began to move out of the inner cities, and instead of buying property, and establishing businesses with their new-found wealth, most chose to go after the house with the picket fence. These blacks utilized the system to get ahead, however most would spend their lives working in a company as a career. White influence became heavy in the 80's, with no Martin, Malcolm, Huey, or a host of other influential blacks from the past, media would now become the social influence within black homes. With television growing, so was the American economy, capitalism was in full swing, and blacks wanted to obtain it. Some choose to take after the cosby's, while some choose to take after new jack city. Television took the place of activists of the past who once had the eyes and ears of the black community. As television depicted and gave black a materialistic outlook that they wanted to obtain. This contributed to the individualistic perspective. At that time most inner-city youth were conspiring to be an athlete, or musician, and by mid-80's a rapper. While black male's role models were consistent with these particular images, the black women on the other hand role models were educated or successful, and with no guidance black women set out to obtain education degrees, and establish long term careers. With the technology era coming into full motion, black women were eager to get ahead and most would seek to obtain this success by any means necessary. They had no choice, with teen pregnancy becoming an epidemic, along with mass incarceration, young black women were left with children, and two options, one to go down and get assistance from the state, or become ambitious and pursue a degree and a career. They became important to black women at this time for a number of reasons. With sports being discriminatory toward woman, black woman would not look to become sports icon or rappers, they set out to become educated. black women had come to identify with one of the major problems of the race, while black man reality was either becoming a rapper, boxer, basketball player, or football player. Once most black male saw that they would not be either of the above, education was the last thing on their mind, they began to drift to a life of crime, by way of drug dealing. The drug epidemic would increase the black on black violence, and now all over the world in inner cities young blacks that lived on the same block were now representing those blocks as their own. Once this dynamic came into play, with the major drug influence, turf wars would kick off and black would now transgress to its number one killer. Now let's focus on the new social conditions that are being implemented, one, the role of the household is beginning to switch with so many black women raising children on their own, she has now become the head of the household. Next came the drugs, black on black violence, and music influence. We watched as the morals and values before the 80's began to fade, and then came new social issues except adding its own social condition, while the ones from the past were still present. The new social influences would be more detrimental than any in the past. With black men at the time failing to obtain an education, they began to become less effect in the home front, anmost became a liability to black women that lived in the inner city, utilizing the impoverished situations to fund their drug expedition's. This exploitation of the black woman placed her in a vulnerable state due to her struggles, and single parenting. Most inner-city women that would support and aid in the dealer expedition were more than likely the ones collecting assistance from the state and chose not to work. The majority of black women that had careers, worked or attended school, would more than likely decline a dealer's offer. The developmental stages of the black child born in the 80's to the two particular subject's we are discussing, would only have the negativity that exist in his home as his or her identification of what life as an adult is. The child's home and environment would determine and develop his or her social cognition. The 80's would also show an epidemic where the sons and daughters that were subject to single parent homes, would eventually grow and have children together. Analyzing the information, one can see the detriment of this type of relationship. Here we have two emotionally deprived children that possibly had no nurturance, guidance or empowerment from their parents, and were now creating a child. With both being emotional imbalances due to lack of dual parenting within the homes, could this be why domestic violence is so high in the inner cities? A large percentage of black children live within homes where the abuse is constant, arguments are daily, and financial stress is a constant reminder. The environment has been lost from any form of consciousness and since our activists and advocates from the past ideologies have diminished, so has the intellectual capacity of our race. Yes, we are more educated than ever, but there is a difference between the educated of the present versus the educated of the past. The educated of the past had less social influence, the social influence of the present has caused a large majority to conform to this influence, which has been fashioned off a capitalistic mentality. The capitalist mentality was created through media depiction, and within this time, blacks lost the energy to fight and the new leaders such as Jesse Jackson and Al Sharpton weren't as influential or charismatic as leaders from the past, plus they had a price. During the 70's blacks lost the identity that was being restored during the 60's and the 80's would reveal that. The black race during this time began to focus on its own individual personal issues, and the race issue was pushed to the back. During the 80's we had no strong black leaders, or movements. As we moved into the 80's even though the consciousness of the black race began to fade, what remained is social oppression, racism, and the victim stance. The one ideology that travels from the 60's to present is the ideology that Malcolm X laid within the inner city, not what EL Hajj El Malik Shabbazz, or any other substantial leaders from the past. Malcolm's ideology was easy to accept because it taught blacks how to blame whites for all their injustices, we began to blame white America for issues that we were fully responsible for. As the drugs hit, we began to allow our communities to go with it. One thing we must understand is that within black community the social condition of the home expands into the community, it doesn't stay isolated. We know that the physical and social component of an environment is created from a mental perspective of most of that group. That mental perspective came by way of a multitude of social influences by way of drugs, and gangs, whether international gangs or local, all gangs were involved in some form of activity that involved drugs. As the drugs moved in at a rapid rate, black family structures were steady declining. "overcrowded housing, poor physical and mental health, despair, post-traumatic stress disorder, family dissolution, teen pregnancy, school dropout, interpersonal violence, crime, and drug and alcohol abuse, among others. These factors help perpetuate disadvantage across generations. Some of these factors are the direct consequences of structural disadvantage. Others involve personal volition, those regarding sexuality, relationships, violence, and illicit drug use. Hence, there appears to be a clear cultural (or subcultural) basis to these behaviors." The environments began to reflect the overall mentality of most. during the 80's up until present, as you go into the major inner cities, you will see rows of abandoned homes, after the other. The homes became abandoned for years on in with no one from the environment taking interest into rebuilding. As the economic wealth of blacks increased, so did the poverty, and this would be utilized to show separation. Black that obtained success were considered middle class and once they reached the stature, the foundation was left where it was. Large percentage of the middle class began to use the current success to combat the economic issue and financial problem with black America that was still pointing the finger at white America. Some black that became middle class were sincere in their delivery to uplift the community, others chose not to touch the issue with fear of tarnishing their image amongst their successors. The media helped capitalism move into the minds of blacks, most were now putting down their gloves, and conforming. This conforming is not to be seen in a negative light, the only issue with it was that blacks that obtained success chose not to support their own, and sell to the highest bidder, the dollar became god in the eyes of most blacks. Some would dispute this; however, we can just look at how the prayers changed, blessings were now considered material gains, everything that blacks began to obtain that signifies success by way of white America, they consider themselves blessed. In the past, prayer was utilized to protect the families and forgive others, that ideology changed also. As the capitalistic mentality began to seep in, blacks began attaching their image to their materialistic gains. No level of intellect was being administered, and most were becoming educated to the systematic component that makes up the economic system in the U.S. The reason being, money was the concern, while most have it transfixed in their mind that poverty is the reason behind blacks' condition, this has been the most enabling element giving to blacks. Poverty is not the issue, we can speak of many ethnic groups that migrate from other countries, coming from 10x worse social conditions than blacks in America, move right into the poverty-stricken areas we complain about, and own a multitude of grocery stores, restaurants, and children are attending college. Poverty is not the issue, we will touch on this later. The mental, social, and cognitive development of blacks by way of cultural disenfranchise has caused them to become victims of conformity by way of social influence to obtain more money. This conformity to a capitalistic mentality with the hope of erasing the impoverished conditions that caused most to lack conscious development into intellect. The lack of conscious development, resulted in the race falling behind, even though the education increased, the intellect and unity fell. As the intellect and unity fell so did the social environment, and once the 80's took course the results would reveal the detriment that the black race faced.

Chapter 28

culture shift

During the 80's crack would take the inner city by storm, adding to the demise that was already spiraling. The biggest surge in the use of the drug occurred during the "crack epidemic," between 1984 and 1990, when the drug spread across American cities. In 1985, the number of people who admitted using cocaine on a routine basis increased from 4.2 million to 5.8 million. By the early 90's black family structures within the inner cities were dismantled. More than half of the pregnancies were conceived by single teenage mothers, and 67% of black families were living within a single home, predominantly headed by a woman. The drug crack would cause a social dilemma that would affect the inner city and remove the trust that was once established amongst blacks. Crack displaced families and added more social problems to the inner city. The long term and short-term effects of crack on an individual are severe and detrimental to one's psychological development. "Crack causes a short-lived, intense high that is immediately followed by the opposite— intense depression, edginess and a craving for more of the drug. People who use it often don't eat or sleep properly. They can experience increased heart rate, muscle spasms and convulsions. The drug can make people feel paranoid, angry, hostile and anxious—even when they aren't high. As we focus on the crack era which consists of the 80's where it took full surface, the black communities suffered the most. Looking at the effects of crack, and focusing on the topic at hand, we understand the concept of being emotionally deprived and lacking the proper nurturance as a child. The text has taught that the social cognition that is developed within a child takes places during the developmental stages between 0-12, we know that as the family structure declined, the children suffer most, and black children were being born under nurtured, and underdeveloped cognitively, and developmentally, furthermore affecting the psychological capacity of the child. During the 80's, the % of black families that were affected by the crack epidemic created a culture shift. Looking at the % that were affected by teenage pregnancy, single parenting, fatherless homes, emotionally deprived, lack of finances we can see how the criminal element in black communities increased. The elements implemented before crack resulted in a surge of subcultures, increase in crime, mass incarceration, hate rhetoric, white guilt, and impoverished conditions. The above condition resulted in 31% of black women being pregnant teenagers during the 70's. As we move through the 80's this number would increase by 23%by the end of 1990.

Focusing on the so-called crack era, we had a surge of black children being born to crack induced mothers, who were then left to live within an emotionally deprived home which were battling the crack addiction, and absent father. Keep in mind the elements that were present beforehand. As crack hit the streets, it eventually created dysfunction within the home. The symptoms of crack would cause a parent to emotionally deprive the child due to the addiction. This addiction increased the crime rate within the black community. The crime became victims of their own as the drugs became king, for the dealers and users. Drug dealers, drug users were now the cultural norm. On the west, where there were once political activists and college education blacks promoting black power; that was replaced by bloods and Crips. In Detroit, and Chicago, GD'S, vice lord, and a slew of other gangs would control the influence that was once held by the nation of Islam and black panthers. On the east, there were now 5%, and Latino gangs. Each of the members would have some involvement in criminal activity that more than likely resulted in the victimizing of their own kind, right from in their own city. On the east, a new birth was merging through hip-hop, rap was now taking the airways and the social influence within the black communities. The black community consciousness began to fade, a surge of rap artists would utilize their music to re-instill that consciousness. The social influence of the black community was now being placed in an awkward position with so many social influences. Black population consist of Christianity, NOI, orthodox Muslim, 5%, vice lord, GD'S, bloods, crips, isrealities, Moors, Pan-africanist, and multiple others. There has to be some prevalence as to why out of all nations, and ethnic groups, why would blacks have so many cultural influences. The researchers Hazel Markus and Shinobu Kitayama have studied how an individual's cultural background affects how they view themselves. People from individualistic cultures are more likely to have an independent view of themselves (they see themselves as separate from others, define themselves based on their personal traits, and see their characteristics as relatively stable and unchanging). On the other hand, people from collectivistic cultures are more likely to have an interdependent view of themselves (they see themselves as connected to others, define themselves in terms of relationships with others, and see their characteristics as more likely to change across different contexts. Cultural influences have affected the black community on a large scale. As different cultures evolved, this changed the social environment within the black communities. Blacks as a group were witnessing a dynamic split. The west coast cultural influences made way for gang culture rising. With bloods and Crip occupying each corner as a territorial ground, the children that were subjected to that said environment have a strong chance of conforming. Example, a child born within an area that consists of predominantly crips, will become a victim of the environmental factors if the child is born to a family that is heavily involved with the gang.

Through multiple cultural influences blacks conformed to gangs instead of consciousness movements which were once relevant in communities of color. Let's look at examples of cultural influence transgressed into generational demise. Let's take Philadelphia, we know that Malcolm became the minister in Philadelphia in the 50's, and during the 60's, movements such as the B.L.A., and MOVE also evolved during this time. During the 80's drug culture made way and one group of predominately Muslim would take philly by storm, the J.B.M. Before Malcolm's influence philly had a large Christian base, by the early 60's, the black community began to convert to the NOI. This conversion came by way of the popularity of Malcolm X. As we moved through the 60's, Malcolm eventually denounced his NOI roots, and began to practice orthodox Muslim. The black community in philly would soon follow, and most converted to orthodox Muslim, as you would see today, Philadelphia is made up of predominantly black Muslim, whom families converted in the 50's, and 60's. Philly has a neighboring influence on Atlantic city, Camden, and other surrounding southern New Jersey cities. Most of these cities are predominantly Muslim based off followers of Malcolm in the 50's. As the generation moved through the decades, and the social condition changed, we watched Philadelphia crime rise. The predominantly Muslim population became known for high crime and violence amongst their own community. Looking at the dynamics of cultural influences and how social environments can triple the effects based on how detriment the social change affects the community. As the areas became flooded with blacks converting to Islam, this brunt about a unified body of people, that were indoctrinated under the same religious pretense. Meaning their cultural, social, and environmental elements should be the same, being that there is no other outer influence involved, unlike for example, you had blood and Crip, this caused a split, however, in Philadelphia, the conscious outlook and religious perspective was the same as the majority. Unfortunately, Philadelphia would in the years to follow the 60's produced a genocidal environment that produces hundreds of murders of black on black crimes by way of the drug culture, which created the street codes, that was forced upon everyone growing up in the said environment. These street codes were utilized to protect the drug trade from being infiltrated by law enforcement. Soon these street codes would affect the civilians living within the environment who feared the dealers, addicts, and gang members. Some people become prisoners of their own homes as the violence increases. Most couldn't enjoy the communities as they once did with fear of bullets flying. This was a hard pill for the older generation that came from the 40's, 50's, and 60's. The behaviors that were being displayed by black male within the community had taken the social environment by storm causing the older generation to witness the demise of the once thriving black communities' that were filled with black unity and a stance against the initial issue which was social injustice and inequality. The older generation watched as the hate that was utilized to fight white oppression was now a hate that was directed at its own kind. Once prominent leaders were not being established, the energy that the community used to fight for rights, became an energy used to destroy their own kind. The quest for financial stability caused the inner city to develop individualistic cultures, geared toward establishing financial success. Each group that was formed produced a criminal element that was geared toward obtaining some type of financial relief. Financial problems as the 70's rolled in affected many cities, especially the ones hit hard by the riots.

With industrial jobs advancing toward a more technological base, Blackmen eventually took on a life of crime. They took on a life of crime all while representing a certain sub-culture that would soon be identified as gangs. Being that poverty was the main stressor, as the drug trade came in, this became the answer to most problems. As the financial and capitalistic mentality became the forefront of black thinking, this would bring about change within not only the social environment, but also the characteristic and personality of individuals. The mentality would now become a capitalistic one. With no leaders, or economic strategy, the drug trade would welcome a new-found wealth in the black community

Chapter 29

Culture is defined as, The beliefs, customs, arts, etc., of a society, group, place, or time. a society that has its own beliefs, ways of life, art, etc. way of thinking, behaving, or working that exists in a place or organization. Looking at how culture is defined, the black race in America cannot identify with the concept of culture such as other ethnic groups. Example, every nationality or ethnic group within the US has their own specific dishes, and restaurants identified as such include west indies, Caribbean's, south America, and so forth. Black in America cultural dishes consist of soul food, which was created during slavery. Each ethnic group has a specific day or parade in which they embrace their culture. This embrace that is displayed is attached emotionally and with pride. Blacks in America have no said attachments to attach to, even though there are African American day parades, however they hardly attended, nor do they take them seriously. One must ask why, why naturally do the black race choose not to attend. It's evident, the natural feeling that other ethnic groups attach to, blacks don't identify with that feeling, so where there is no emotion, there is no attachment. The cultural definition has yet to be understood within the black community. Within the black community we have tried to attach to African custom, but in all actuality, what are we truly attaching to. Most black American have no recollection into what culture they distinguish from, or what country they are from. Within Africa there are thousands of dialects and an abundance of cultures that differentiate from each other. Nigerians operate differently than natives from Kenya and so forth, however in America they represent the continent of Africa with an attachment to a specific culture. What binds Africans of different cultures is they have the same economic agenda; therefore, cultural perspective doesn't get in the way of business. Just as most ethnic groups from other countries that migrate to the states, they all have the same economic, and educational motive. The cultural perspectives that exist within each establish a foundation that develops the child to succeed. The difference within the developmental stages of most children, in comparison to black children, is the emotional support. As we identify that there are immigrants that migrate and live within the same environment as black Americans, however they still strive and have a high ratio of success. The cultural perspective is important to the developmental stages because the culture is what creates the social environment which is designed off the social cognition and perception of the majority. For years blacks have strived to find their place in the east, by converting to Muslim or attaching to African customs. This is a cry out for a place and an identification. With blacks losing hope in Christianity due to the social injustice that was implemented, and based on how blacks were converted to Christianity, most sought out to find faith and acceptance in other religions and cultures. The search is what caused the split, and the fact that we as a people have no culture to attach too, we are quick to conform, for the sake of not feeling lost, especially if you are conscious. Looking at the perspective of culture, blacks neglect its culture that exists right here in America. Instead of creating a culture based on our art, music, and history, instead we are searching out for other cultures to identify our origin. The cultural perspectives of blacks must first be consciously established here first, before it can search out to find its African origin. Culture is important to the social development of a group or race. Blacks have no true cultural perspectives, we adopt other ethnic groups' cultural and social views. When we look at culture, culture is based on historic fact and documented successes, and belief that establish a group. These beliefs are the perspective that govern the attitude and perspectives of its people, even if they stray as they become adults, their culture will still exist within their ethnic background, even when the religious views change. Let's analyze some forms of how culture is defined, "Culture in its broadest sense is cultivated behavior; that is the totality of a person's learned, accumulated experience which is socially transmitted, or more briefly, behavior through social learning." Looking at the definition presented above, we can identify with culture not fully defined by religion, that's evident with how some Muslim live in India, versus Muslims in Arabia, the religion is the same, but the culture is different. Culture becomes cultivated behavior, which is learned through social perception, and social learning of the same group of people. Looking at the black race, how would we define our culture? I'll explain to you how we identify our culture and how it is a hindrance and a social dilemma that persists to add invites to the issue at hand. take black history month. You can identify this as part of our culture because we embrace it each year, however the media controls how it is depicted, unfortunately it shouldn't exist, this is the psychological programming that conflicts with the conscious development within the black population. How can you sum your history up in one month. Our culture creates a mentality of despair, hopelessness, and deferred dreams. Our culture lies at the root of slavery, lynching, KKK, riots, police brutality, teenage pregnancy, single parenting, poverty, lack of financial planning, the defamation of character of past and present leaders, drugs, alcohol, and the worst of all, nonsupport of black owned businesses. These above variables make up our culture, which causes a sense of hopelessness. What is sad is that just within the 1900's, we can re-create a culture of a slew of positive movements of musicians, artists, writers, scholars, inventors, educators, and poets. Our culture has created individualism that transgresses into hate and envy of one another. The individualistic perspective that has become the mindset of a large percent of blacks, has contributed to the constant issue in family and relationships at present. Blacks are scrutinized by each other and criticized by one another.

For example, Barack Obama is elected president, and the majority of so-called activists and scholars can and will look for more dirt or ways to discredit him more than they will bushes and Reagan. That's not the point, the point is how the black race are quick to lose hope on their own, when they are truly aware of how the executive office works. This form of behavior does not raise the consciousness of the race, it destroys it. Therefore, our culture has distorted and desolate views that focus on the negative more so then the positive. This attitude became prevalent in the race during the 80's to present. With no culture to guide us, nor reestablishing a foundation, that would all end for the worst. The new social element that would surface would be rap. The culture of black America would now rely on its music to restore the image. With no positive influence in the 70's midway through the 80's rap would infiltrate the ears and consciousness of black America, this would be the time where music would depict a social condition that was destroying a race.

Chapter 30

With the cultural influence up for grabs, the mid 80's made way for rap, artists such as Kurtis Blow, Run DMC, grandmaster flash, and others made way for artists that would take rap to the next plateau. Krs-1, Rakim, Big Daddy Kane, LLCOOLJ, and public enemies would create the cultural perspective for the black race. the rap culture became the black culture, and furthermore began to affect the social perspective. With artists such as Krs-1 with songs such as self-destruction, and you must learn lyrics that ignited the consciousness within the black youth giving them a different perspective versus what was seen in the community. In the 70's and 80's was a dark time for the black race with no socially conscious leaders to restore the black mindset that existed in years past. P.E made song such as fight the power and express yourself, these songs were mirror images of the 60's fight the power movement, and slavery. P.E. attacked the radical element in which was designed by Malcolm under the nation of Islam. Rakim on the other hand added lyrics that expressed his influential up bringing within the nation of 5% which was a movement that branched of the nation of Islam. As the late 80's gave inner city youth hope, and with Michael Jordan being at the height of his career, inner city youth looked to be either rappers, or sports players. Unfortunately, players like Barkley chose not to be identified as a role model. Movies such as Jungle fever, and do the right thing were now being displayed, and Spike Lee was now involved in restoring the black consciousness that had been at a standstill for at least 15 years. The images that rappers began to display began to influence the inner city, and with the drug trade brewing, this would be a recipe for disaster. Just as rap was looked at as a positive, straight out of Compton would change the game of rap forever, and with that would restore the element that was already brewing. With N.W.A. receiving national buzz, the money they received off their first album caused record executives to evaluate the music they were putting out. NWA showed record companies the potential that rap had. As gangster rap became the focal point of record executives now, music such as Krs-1, Rakim, and so forth would now be music of the past. As gangster rap on the west depicted Blood, Crip, LAPD, and so forth, the east would give a vivid image of its streets, mixed with a 5% dialect, music now on the east began to signify cars, clothes, jewelry, drugs, and violence. The conscious rap of the past was not producing so-called gangster rap. The new form of rap that was taking the airways was also affecting the social environment within the black communities. Cars, clothes, and jewelry worn by rappers became an admiration of young emotional deprived black males. These three elements; emotional deprivation, poverty, and rap would force young black male to venture out into drug sales. The rap image mixed with what young black youth see on their street corners were black male lounges on corners sitting on crates occupying space to operate drug sales. The men on these corners driving expensive cars, jewelry and expensive clothing are creating social influence on the inner city youth. The drug dealers look like the rappers, therefore, this admiration for the drug dealers comes by way of wanting to look like a rapper. By being emotionally deprived, kids can identify with rappers as the only success for blacks. With the drug trade and rap music taking flight, the culture of the inner city began to invade the suburban areas. Blacks felt as though rap was their own creation that no one could steal. The youth embraced rappers that illuminated their life and the social condition that followed. Rap music in the 80's reflected on the restoration of consciousness and the equal stance in unity. The 90's would change that; rap artists were now glorifying criminal acts and violence against its own kind. Music in the west discussed gang violence, but also glorified it. Rap became a form of indoctrination, reason being as youth attached to rappers, the words of their music they began to mimic and repeat verbatim. This became the social influence within the urban city. Youth began to identify with the clothing, jewelry, and cars. To the youth this signified success, and with music videos becoming a headline in the 90's, the influence from the streets to the music began to display heavily. The depiction in videos glorified the materialistic aspects of life, but not the economic, therefore sending a false message, furthermore affecting the progression of the race.

158

Blacks are one of the biggest consumers in the world but own so little in comparison to other ethnic groups. We watched lines of children and adults stand outside the sneaker store awaiting to buy a pair of sneakers. Materialism became an attraction to youth because it signified money, and success amongst their peers. However, what should be looked at is the mentality that is displaying the behavior. Example, a pair of Jordan's, depending on the make can cost 300$, this amount is a signification of success. Materialism influenced the minds of the youth and assisted in their venture into the drug world. Within an inner city, by the mid 90's most corners were occupied by dealers and addicts. The daily traffic consists of children going to school, playing, drug selling, violence, police presence, and alcoholics. Each corner is a representation of a household within that area. The members that occupy each corner more than likely were born and raised in that area. The cycle repeats, and a high percentage will succumb to the environment. As the years passed on, there was a strong correlation between the increase in violent music, and an increase in crime within the inner cities. By late 90's, all music that was being produced was representing a criminal element. Feuds kicked off between east and west coast rappers resulting in death. Music artists were, while signed, still committed crimes and involved in a criminal element that was expressed in their music and this pushed the indoctrinated into the youth. The early 2000's would increase the violence and the temperament within black youth. The incarceration rate tripled and drug offenses for black males were through the roof. In the early 2000's, a new wave was entering the east coast, bloods and Crips were now taking the influence of the east. In the tri-state, NY, NJ, and Conn, bloods and crips were now becoming the major influence of the inner-city youth city such as Newark, Paterson, Jersey City and a host of other inner cities on the east, and eventually flooding in the south. By early 2000's bloods and crips populated the entire country, every city that consisted of high populated blacks had some percentage of its youth conform to blood or crip. The connection from east, west, south, and north showed a unity that was unknown to the black race. These two sub-cultures have recruited more black youth than any organization known to the black race in America. 47 years to the present 2017, bloods and crips have been within inner cities communities. These movements have outlasted the panthers, the civil rights movement, panAfrican, and UNIA. No other organization, neither the Nation of Islam has ever had this much social influence on the inner-city youth. Inner cities were taken by storm with the new sub-cultures that travel from the west. As the gang infiltration began to substantiate, the violence on the east began to rise. Blood and crip violence began to take the inner city by storm, as the numbers increased, so did the murders. Territories were named after particular gangs, and if you were not affiliated, you could not be involved in the criminal finances that transpired in particular territories. In the 2000's, cities such as Newark, Philly, Detroit, Chicago, New Orleans, Miami, Atlanta, the Carolinas, and a slew of other cities were all socially influenced by gang culture. Generations have become born into the gangs, due to parents' affiliation. High schools, and middle schools began to feel the presence of gang pressure from its teenagers, especially in the west, and in Chicago. These particular areas have had major gang infiltration into the high school and middle school, furthermore resulting in gang wars right on school property. The culture for the youth became wrapped around music and gang influence. Soon, the music began to display the gang culture. Rappers were representing their gang and wearing their colors proudly in music videos all while throwing up gang signs. The media image became the mindset of the youth, and the music displayed it. At present 2017, over a process of 100 years, the above that has been discussed has shaped and molded the consciousness of black youth, and the depiction has created the image of the black race. We have watched our minds strive to establish a place, but our heart never settles. The emotional deprivation by way of neglect develops emotional imbalances. Emotionally and developmentally a large percentage of the black race are behind. On the flip side, the other percentage that are educated are wrapped into a career that has no economic substance, only financial stability, but that doesn't rid the day to day struggles. With the educated blacks being just that, we have lost the intellectual capacity to establish unity and support each other. By this, this leaves the less fortunate to succumb to environmental factors. Culture has been a big issue within the black race, the culture must be restored in a different light, not based on someone else's doctrine of how you should define your culture. The cultural influence of music has placed our present generation in far worse condition than of the past. Drugs, and music influence are going hand and hand, the destruction is increasing and black on black crime is climbing. Example, by the mid 2000's, the south became the influence, and with them came the social elements that made up those particular cities. Rappers from the south glorified using Zaynax, promethazine, codeines, percocets, alcohol, mollies, and marijuana. The weapon they glorified in the south was the chopper, also known as the AK47. As the south became the musical influence, the east began to adopt their ways, and indulge in the same criminal and drug element as the south. AK47 started to be utilized in the east and north during drug wars, turf disputes, and gang wars which are all three different forms of violence against a so-called opposition. The evidence of music influence is persistent and shows strongly in young black male. From 1965 we watched the mentality shift from black power, to gang sub- cultural influence. From 1964, and back the only influence was Christianity, and a small number of NOI followers. Most movements from 1970 back had a Christian religious overtone. Other thoughts to factor in, the police brutality, white hate crime, discrimination, racism, injustice, and inequality was worst from 1965 back. Looking forward, 1965 to present, all factors were still present, but not to the extent as it was prior to. Mass incarceration has now become a choice within the developmental stages of young black males raised in urban environments. The social environment has presented the drug culture as a form of obtaining wealth for a large percent of young black youth. Most black males are raised in predominantly woman raised homes so without the father's presence to grant the equal balance of emotional nurturance, the child succumbs to the outside environment. The outside environment consists of gangs, drugs and constant despair. This would define the fact why so many young black male conform to gangs. At present with a large percentage of young black males between the ages of 14-24, fathers have a strong chance of being affiliated with one of the above sub-cultures. Some youth may join gangs to draw connections to their fathers who are also affiliated with the same sub-culture. A direct result of the blind leading the blind, and the reason for the increase in black on black crime. The mindset has not changed therefore the elements that create it remain the same, furthermore causing social dilemmas within inner cities.

Chapter 31

Black women suffered the most throughout this period, as well as contributed a lot to it also. Mass incarceration was steadily inclining, while the black family structure was declining. As mass incarceration began to affect the inner city, women faced more life obstacles than expected. As the 50's and 60's stood strong with two parent family structures, the black woman was able to enforce the emotional support the family needed to remain balanced through the struggle. In some homes the women held jobs also, but with the man present, they were able to still maintain the homes, and the emotional nurturance needed for the children to develop properly. With the man present, the woman was able to take on the role needed, and the children were able to stay children. What that means is that as homes became fatherless, the older children were forced to take on the role as a guardian over the younger sibling while the mother was working. Black women faced a double standard, along with a double consciousness. While black woman was subjected to the same conditions as the black man, they also were subject to the discrimination that came with being a woman. This affected the black woman that was raising children alone. Working minimum jobs, sometimes two and three, women were forced to leave the children home alone, furthermore, remove the emotional nurturance that was once within the homes. With older children taking on roles of guardianship over the younger sibling, this forces the older children to take on responsibilities that he or she was not capable of. Due to the lack of the father's presence, black woman had no choice in the matter. Working long hours, and some even attending school, by the time the mother would come home, she would be too tired to cater fully emotionally to her child, and if she has more than one, the situation worsens. Black woman took the short end of the stick and was forced to pick up the slack of the fathers. During the 1900's, black America never truly focused on the extent in which the black woman played within the role of society. With no strong leadership influence, black women were falsely represented. Most black women had no significant role models due to gender biases. sports for black women were unheard of until the 90's. black men had images to follow, their hope lies in being a professional sports figure, then later the idea of being rappers came into play. Even in rap, women have never had a strong significant place. With all the avenues black men were finally being able to break through, the woman sat in the back and patiently waited to be acknowledged. As the black man began to weaken, the black woman began to strengthen, sadly in most cases it was by force, due to incompetent parenting on the fathers' part. As the 90's rolled in, the incarceration rate for black men was climbing, along with teenage pregnancy, and single parenting. The 90's would be defined as the birth of the phenomenon woman, which was the independent woman. This woman represented the woman that stood her ground and handled her business in a male dominant economic environment. This was a theme song for black women, which came by way of their new independence due to the weakening of the black man. As the 90's rolled in, women were able to make their way. With most pursuing degrees, and careers that set their lives straight, the more they felt the black man was not needed. It wouldn't be odd to see how they can come to think like that, if you raise your child, or children alone with no assistance, your trials, tribulation, and struggle will make you develop this outlook. As black women began to rise, the system became more geared to assist. black women were not only black, but they were women, which made them a double minority. As the years passed, and the incarceration of black men steadily increased, the black woman independence also increased. With this increase, this caused some black women to look down on black men that didn't have prestigious degrees, or financial status. The psychological condition is as follows, as the years traveled on, black men began to leave the homes at a rapid rate, some were not leaving the homes, they choose not to even assist in raising the child due to immaturity. As this becomes the norm within an environment, as each woman can identify with the same situation as the next, this will form a negative outlook, which then will become an overview of a black man. I say because, some black woman focuses on status as the most deterring factor, with black men that are not raised as the black man growing up in single parenting poverty, and violence ridden areas, they tend to use forms of discrimination against this black man. The reason being is because 85% of the time, the men that are not assisting in their child's life come from broken, single parent homes. This is due to lack of emotional nurturance, and irresponsibility that comes by way of being underdeveloped. This way of thinking becomes the automatic thinking of a person because this is what their environment has led them to believe. If 5 female friends have children by men that come from the said environment, and 3 out of 5 of the children fathers are not present, in some cases all 5 may not be present, or possibly just been released, the variables vary. Situations such as this are what causes women to look at black men from this environment in this manner. statistics can possibly show that most children with absent fathers, a large percentage of the children fathers come from impoverished areas. Women identify with this, and this is what causes them to form negative outlooks within some black men. Their emotional attachment to their struggle with their kids, causes them to reflect on times where if the fathers could've assisted, they wouldn't be forced in a financial jam. Financial stress for some women brings on depression, that depression causes the woman to emotionally deprive the children even more. Depression is common within the inner city. Families endure constant struggles for food, clothing and shelter. As we moved through the 1900's, we can look at women's demeanor from past to present. The demeanors of women of the past are different from women of the present because present women take on more, and black men are much more responsible and supportive. As the responsibility and support of the man dwindled, so did the attitude and perspectives of women. By the 70's, black women were still receiving a substernal amount of support from their children's fathers. Unfortunately, by the 80's, this would fade and the struggle that black women endured would create the mindset of the independent woman. Looking at history, we can see how this was coming into play throughout the decades, up to present 2017. Sadly, to say, a new social element that will affect the black community is the removal of big momma. Big momma signifies the grandmother that displays an insurmountable level of strength while raising the family. This grandmother consists of women over 50 years old at present, the grandmothers are now as young as 35, sadly some of the young grandmothers are product of broken single parent homes, and never received the proper emotional nurturance due to absentee fathers. As the grandmothers become younger, this removes the southern background that bonded families together. The present younger grandmothers are products of their environment and do not have the same sense of moral value as black women of the past. So, what we are witnessing is this, in 1991, 54 percent of black children were born to single teenage mothers. Fast forward, 2017, the same issues are present, and now the daughter and sons of the teenage mothers in early 90's are now parents, making them grandmothers. So the mentality and social conditions that developed teenage pregnancy, is the same element that are developing younger grandmothers that lack the proper nurturance and emotional balance to raise children, resulting in black on black crime.

Chapter 32

black on black crime and its origin

Black on black crime has reached an all-time high within the past few years. Inner cities that consist of high gang violence and drug traffic have shown that blacks have increased the violence amongst one another. Cities such as Newark, Chicago, Detroit, New Orleans, Philadelphia, and others have seen an increase within black on black crime. Over the past few years things have begun to reach astronomical numbers that reflect a social complexity, and social condition that caused a converse oppression. Black male violence amongst each other derives from various conflicts that result in killing one another. Crimes that young black male inflict on their own consist of murder, robbery, burglary, violence, extortion, and drugs. With gang violence taking over during the 80's, the mentality eventually affected the community. Non-gang members found themselves now protecting themselves from gang members and police. As drugs took over the community and began to fund most urban families, young black males began to fall victim to gangs and drugs at a rapid rate. Music became a prominent influence during this time, promoting drugs and violence, but worst of all was the depiction of black women. By the 90's, communities consisted of violence, and music that promoted the violence as it was being inflicted on its own. This psychologically changed the mindset of black youth. A large percentage of the music assisted in devaluing black consciousness, and shaping the street code, and street mentality. This mentality progressed and created the increase in black on black crime. With drugs and violence at every corner, non-gang members would soon develop the same mentality as gang members with the purpose of protection. Social pressure was at an all-time high for young black males conforming to gang violence, or gang mentality. Women, teenagers preferably would eventually fall for the black males that socially adjusted to this way of thinking. With no leaders in play, gang leaders, drug dealers and hip-hop became the culture. As the years progressed, the mentality began to set, and crime rose, and by the mid 90's, black on black crime was becoming an issue. One circumstance that display the beginning of black on black crime was in, "During a meeting of the Black Student Union at UCLA's Campbell Hall on January 17, 1969, Bunchy Carter and another BPP member named John Huggins were heard making derogatory comments about Ron Karenga, the head of Organization US. Other accounts mention a heated argument between US members and Panther Elaine Brown. An altercation ensued during which Carter and Huggins were shot to death." The mentality began to develop in the 70's, the 80's it began to reveal itself, the 90's it became identified as an epidemic, and by the 2000's it was full fledged. Different time frames display black on black crime at different levels. During the 80's cities like Harlem, Bronx, Brooklyn, Queens, and Manhattan saw the drug trade take off. As the drug trade took off in inner cities, so did the crime, murder in particular. As the economic plight for blacks worsened, the criminal element became more prevalent. "From 1980 to 2008, the number of people incarcerated in America quadrupled-from roughly 500,000 to 2.3 million people Today, the US is 5% of the World population and has 25% of world prisoners. Combining the number of people in prison and jail with those under parole or probation supervision, 1 in every 31 adults, or 3.2 percent of the population is under some form of correctional control." a state or process in which persons, groups, or cultures lose or do not have communication or cooperation with one another, often resulting in open conflict this is defined as social isolation from a sociological outlook. Social isolation, Isolation can increase feelings of loneliness and depression, fear of other people, or create a negative self-image. There is a realization in the individual that their isolating is not 'normal behavior' and can create the feeling that there is a whole world going on to which they do not belong or are unable to be a part of. As inferiority set in, inner city black became socially isolated to their environment, furthermore, inflicting their anger and aggression on one another. This aggression, and hunger for money mixed with gangs and gang mentality began to inflict their oppressive manner on the communities. Black on black violence became the communities' ways of releasing its pent-up anger and aggression.

Chapter 33

anatomy of violence

Violence is defined as aggressive behavior with bodily harm caused by an oppressive force. "As a man thinks in his heart, so is he."

Violence has always been a part of human origin because of our iniquity nature (Rom. 3:23). Nonetheless up-to-date families are exposed to even more violence than prior generations because of the media depiction. Looking at the black community violence became prevalent against their own during the late 70's to present. Analyzing the history of America and violence, we can depict how this temperament can be relevant within a sample of the total population. America was built off crimes that are now utilized to punish minorities, and its own population. Crimes that were committed amongst people within America, are now the crimes that inner cities are being charged and imprisoned for. Unfortunately, these crimes are directed at their own. Crimes that make up blacks that are incarcerated are, robbery, murder, extortion, drug dealing, home invasion, stolen car, and burglary. Analyzing the above crimes, one should see that each crime is driven by the same motivating factors. That motivating factor is the dollar. The dollar for inner cities families have proven to represent GOD, with constant depression and injustice, poverty within the inner city has made the dollar more prevalent than religion. This evidence is shown based on what is considered a blessing. Most people of religion identify blessing with something that supports a better financial situation. I utilize this concept for one particular reason, that is to identify with capitalism and how it has created the epidemic of black on black crime, and a justice system that is designed to devalue the black population.

Looking at the concept of violence and how it's defined, we would have to look at criminal behavior that consists of violence, and look at the whole concept of criminal behavior. Psychology defines criminal behavior as a progression into anti-personality disorder. I say progression because, within psychology, there are behaviors that must be seen before the age of adulthood to define antisocial personality disorder. One disorder that is an on-set for anti-personality disorder is conduct disorder. dysfunction at the developmental stage of development that consist of, trauma, psychological abuse, alcohol abuse in the home, drug abuse, sexual abuse, emotional neglect, and environment. An example, a child may be emotionally neglected within the home, and feel the lack of love, and connection to family. This same individual, living in an environment where gang affiliation is high, the likelihood of that child joining a gang is high. Within that gang, he can build the emotional connection, and acceptance he never receives in the house. There are factors, for example, if a person is lacking in the house, and the environment presents a resource that provides the missing element from the home, a person will go to the environment for that resource. Take the same child that joins a gang at 13, if the home he lives in lacks the necessary food needed to sustain hunger, he will go to the environment for that resource. In most environments where there is heavy gang presence, there are drugs there also. The drugs will be utilized to provide the resource missing in the home. This is nature versus nurture. My reason for explaining this is to show how crimes, and violent behavior is socially constructed to place minorities in a position to fill prisons and utilize the 13th amendment. Let's analyze the child at present. He is currently involved with a gang and selling drugs. The joining of the gang came by way of emotional, and psychological neglect that developed in the home. The gang is what provides the emotional connection because they are all victims of the same circumstances, some worse than others. The same child that joins the gang, receives access to drugs. The home that the child comes from lacks enough financial support for food and clothing, leaving drug selling as the option since it's a resource provided by the gang. In return the child fills the void that was missing in the home. The developmental stages, or Piaget preoperational stage of development which is between 2-7, is defined as the crucial moment in a children's life. what they endure in that time frame shapes their perception.

Looking at the child, we can see why he joined a gang and sold drugs. Now let's add a few other variables to differentiate between certain children. Let's say the same child home consists of a single mother, 3 siblings, and a boyfriend in the house that is not the father. If domestic violence is high in this same home, the child may pick up an aggressive, and violent temperament which will be displayed in the classroom. The child will then show behaviors in the classroom conducive to conduct disorder. This consists of acting out, disrespecting classmates, and teachers, as well as poor performance in school. The result of the child's behavior in school is caused by the events taking place in the home. Another factor is physical abuse, if the child is physically abused in the home, along with domestic violence, lack of emotional support, lack of adequate food and clothing, and physically abused, the chances of him becoming violent, gang related, drug dealer, and violent offender are high.

Next let's analyze the definition of crime, and acts that consist of crimes. According to the black's law dictionary, A crime is an act committed or omitted, in violation of a public law, either forbidding or commanding it; a breach or violation of some public right or duty due to a whole community, considered as a community. In its social aggregate capacity, as distinguished from a civil injury. Crimes consist of: robbery, shoplifting, burglary, home invasion, carjacking, murder, rape, property crimes, and drug dealing. Looking at all the crimes mentioned, they all tie in somehow. Each crime has a component in search of a satisfaction to relieve a stressor. All tie into money, power, and dominance. Men are prone to seek power and dominance, which leads to money. Money assists in providing one resource needed to maintain day to day life. For each criminal behavior, there is a motive, a psychological push motive which motivates one to commit a crime. The crimes are not just tied in psychological, they are also tied in physiological. The physiology consists of day to day needs to maintain the value of life. For one to maintain the value of life, the needs consist of food, clothing and shelter. When these three components are not met, it affects physiologically and psychologically. Example of physiological: the need to eat is important to sustain day to day needs to restore energy from food, water, and salt. A lack of these results in hunger which creates hormones to secret such as ghrelin, which comes from a lack of nutrients in the body and is signaling for it to be restored. The longer a person goes with this need unfulfilled, the more his or her behavior changes. No food in the house, the next step is the environment. Youth are frequently arrested for shoplifting. Shoplifting provides a need, which is money for food to restore psychological and physiological needs. The person that can't find food in the house will either steal it, rob for the money, sell drugs, or burglary for goods to turn into money, which provides a need.

Economics is the driving force to criminal behavior. The physiological need to suppress one's hunger can led to murder, robbery, burglary shoplifting, or whatever contributes to suppress the feeling of hunger. Hunger affects one's behavior and can lead to impulsive behavior. The hungrier person is, the less empathetic they become, in some cases were murder is the result, there is no empathy involved.

Looking at what is presented, crime would be socially constructed. How, one way is through analyzing the social institutes, and lack of adequate support and funding from the federal government. School systems have outdated books, and information, lack of health care, and proper nutritional values. Within the black communities, poverty is the driving force to criminal behavior. Living in the worst condition, and no support from the federal government places poverty as a motivating factor for criminal behavior. Socially blacks are disabled from receiving sufficient financial opportunity which results in poverty. Through socially constructed laws, and policies, blacks are placed at a disadvantage. This disadvantage affects the home, leading to dysfunction within the home. Other leading factors to deal with the issues are drug usage, and alcoholism as a coping mechanism for the distress. This distress leads to depression, and anger. The home that possesses the above issues, has a dynamic effect on the children developmentally. In black inner cities, the environment is a correlation to the home. Homes that lack the necessities, create criminally defined environments which are socially constructed through racist and discriminatory laws and policies. These laws and policies are socially unequal, and lack productivity conducive to black advancement.

Social policies that inflicted systematic racism are also responsible for the vast development of prisons that rose between 1980-2000. As the prison industry rose, so did the severity of criminal laws. Between 1965-1975, crime began to rise. The crime that was being committed was to feed families and provide finances for the homes. Just as crime begins to rise we watch Nixons war on drugs take flight, followed by Reagan, and later on Clinton. The laws that were produced created social dilemmas in black communities. From the year 1965-1970, there were a total of 750 riots. The riots destroyed businesses, which took unemployment up; in the same years, an influx of southern blacks migrated to northern cities and overpopulated them. The overpopulation mixed with unemployment creates tension and frustration, and possible high levels of depression within black homes. Within the same years we watched Martin Luther King, and Malcom X become assassinated. These factors contribute to the development of blacks as a whole. As the times changed, the mentality shifted to a more militarized fashion led by the black power movement. These issues caused many stressors within the communities, along with the lack of adequate finances, and jobs. By the middle of the 70's drugs began to invade the community and single parent homes began to take rise. With criminal laws being implemented, and financial struggles, blacks began to go to jail at a vast rate. This vast rate began to send black males to jail, forcing women to fend for children on their own. As the crack epidemic hit, communities took a swing.

The psychological component to identify with is how things were systematically done. Blacks lacked resources, due to circumstances created from the riots, and socially constructed laws. This in return causes money to be scarce, and creates stress which in return leads to action. Nature versus nurture. The government systematically disenfranchised blacks causing them to result in criminal behavior to feed their families. As the criminal behavior began to elevate, laws were passed that systematically targeted blacks, and imprisoned them for non-violent offenses, and crimes that whites would receive probation for, blacks received harsh time, that resulted in felonies. In response to felonies, once convicted, you lack social privileges to assist in your transition, therefore most go back to what they know which explains the high recidivism rate. As the criminal behavior grew so did the prison industry. In California alone between 1980-2000, 25 prisons were built, and at least 15 were private prisons. The war on drugs was a way to increase laws, reinforce police departments, and build the prison system.

Chapter 34

Here is something to analyze

Nixon and Reagan are responsible for the war on drugs policies. Both were heavily invested in politics in California. Nixon was senator of California from 1947-1953, and Reagan was governor of California from 1967-1975. Nixon became president in 1969 and launched the war on drugs that same year. Nixon ended office in 1974, and Reagan became president in 1981-1989. The biggest surge of crack landed in south central Los Angeles in the 70's. the 80's would be the year drugs took off, coincidentally, Reagan funded the contras, a military group in Nicaragua that was heavily funded by cocaine. In the process of this he was accused of making a arm deal with a Iran, terrorist group. The U.S. government allocated 30million for weapons, but 18 million of the 30 million went to the contras. Now, the biggest crack surge, which is defined as the crack epidemic, took place between 1984-1990, the Iran contra scandal which 18 million of 30 million went to a military group funded by cocaine took place between 1985-1987. Crack hit the west coast first, coincidentally, Nixon ex-senator from California, Reagan, ex-governor from California both promoted the war on drug policies. Reagan gave 18 million to Contras who was funded by cocaine, mysteriously at this same time the crack epidemic takes flight landing in California. Next, we have to look at, between 1980-2000, California built 25 prisons, and increased their prison pop by 478%. Can we say this was systematically done, and conspired by Reagan and Nixon? There is no fact leading to say they were conspiring to disenfranchise black with their policies, and assistance with the Contras, unfortunately it appears that way.

The socially constructed political policies help establish a caste system that at present has places blacks as the highest group incarcerated. At present there are over 2 million people incarcerated.

Between 1980 and 2015, the number of people incarcerated in America increased from roughly 500,000 to over 2.2 million. Today, the United States makes up about 5% of the world's population and has 21% of the world's prisoners.1 in every 37 adults in the United States, or 2.7% of the adult population, is under some form of correctional supervision. In 2014, African Americans constituted 2.3 million, or 34%, of the total 6.8 million correctional population. African Americans are incarcerated at more than 5 times the rate of whites. The imprisonment rate for African American women is twice that of white women. Nationwide, African American children represent 32% of children who are arrested, 42% of children who are detained, and 52% of children whose cases are judicially waived to criminal court. Though African Americans and Hispanics make up approximately 32% of the US population, they comprised 56% of all incarcerated people in 2015. If African Americans and Hispanics were incarcerated at the same rates as whites, prison and jail populations would decline by almost 40%n the 2015 National Survey on Drug Use and Health, about 17 million whites and 4 million African Americans reported having used an illicit drug within the last month. African Americans and whites use drugs at similar rates, but the imprisonment rate of African Americans for drug charges is almost 6 times that of whites. African Americans represent 12.5% of illicit drug users, but 29% of those arrested for drug offenses and 33% of those incarcerated in state facilities for drug offenses. Effects of IncarcerationA criminal record can reduce the likelihood of a callback or job offer by nearly 50 percent. The negative impact of a criminal record is twice as large for African American applicants. Infectious diseases are highly concentrated in corrections facilities: 15% of jail inmates and 22% of prisoners – compared to 5% of the general population – reported ever having tuberculosis, Hepatitis B and C, HIV/AIDS, or other STDs. In 2012 alone, the United States spent nearly $81 billion on corrections. Spending on prisons and jails has increased at triple the rate of spending on Pre-K-12 public education in the last thirty years.

Through the time 970-2000, we watched the U.S becoming the country with the highest incarceration rate. Between the above years, criminal law policy developed that gave birth to mass incarceration. The policies created were designed to decrease the drug traffic that was possibly responsible for the increase in crime. Between 965-975, crime rates had risen at tremendous rate which helped develop the war on drugs policy that was birthed by Nixon, and later continued by Reagan, and Clinton. . These policies called for extreme policing, and laws that would disenfranchise black families. The policies not only disenfranchised black, it created a caste system for black families.

Chapter 35

War on Minorities

The war on drugs was a political ploy to marginalize African Americans and establish mass incarceration for the purpose of free labor. Nixon established the war on drugs as a running platform in the 60's. As Nixon initiated the war on drugs, Reagan picked up where he left off, followed by Clinton. This platform opened the doors for criminal law policies in the future. The criminal law policies affected African American communities and removed large amounts of black father's out of homes. The war on drugs policy brought forth a new law enforcement agency to combat the recent drug epidemic. The DEA came into play in 1973 to assist in the so-called drug epidemic that was arising. Lloyd Stephens defines the war on drugs policies as more harmful than beneficial. Stephen defined the policy as culturally violence targeted at minorities and black. The policy targeted non violent offenders who were addicted to the drugs. This policy also established policies and political laws to come. Jails, institutions, rehabs, militarized police forces, and racial disparities took aim. (Steffen, L. (2018).

The years following, we would watch the Rockefeller law, three strike law, and Clinton's crime bill specifically target African Americans. In lieu of these crime bills, and the war on drugs; African American communities were suffering from unemployment due to the riots between 1965-1970, 750 total riots. In response to the unemployment, the 70's and 80's we watched drugs take over the communities. States that adopted the laws developed from the war on drugs, their prison population increased tremendously. California prison population increased nearly 500% between 1977 and 1998. (J.Simone 2014). This was systematic racism, and a political plight to disenfranchise African Americans and establish the caste system. The three strikes law had a major impact on the black community. California felt it the most between the years 1980-2000, California built 22 prisons, when prior to 1980, they only had 12. . (J.Simone2014)

The criminal law policies that came by way of the War on drugs, was a political ploy to disenfranchise minorities.

Chapter 36

Three Strikes Laws

The three strikes law was established 1993, by 1996, 25 states had adopted the law. Washington D.C. was the first followed by California. Just as the three strike laws were being implemented, in 1994 Bill Clinton would sign the violent crime control and law enforcement act. Each of these policies increased the prison population and criminalized black neighborhoods and made these areas the main target of law enforcement. . (Barnes 2010). As the drug epidemic became a focus of politicians during the 70's and 80's, violent crime and property crime began to increase. The nation's response was harsher sentences, and zero tolerance on felons. Politician argued that statutes would deter and incapacitate high rate recidivism and result in lowering crime.(Stolzenberg Dalessio 1997) crime rates did fall after the Three Strikes law went into effect, analysts expressed concern that the statute might negatively impact racial and ethnic minority groups . (Barnes, S 2010). The California penal system utilized the three strikes law as a tool to increase incarceration, while the 22 prisons were being built between 1980-2000. As the prison population increased, so did migrating immigrants. Over the last three decades, California has had a large influx of migrants, by mid1990's, California had 8 million immigrants, representing one in four state residents, and 1/3 of all immigrants in the US. (S.Camarota1998) .immigrants composed of the second largest percentage of prisoners.

Three Strikes Laws

Three strikes laws displayed racial disparities that were evident. In California, African Americans make up 6.5% of the population, and 30% of the prison population. 36% of second strikers are African American, and 45% of third strikers. Latino population in California is 32.5% as a whole, 36% of the prison population, and 32% of strikers. (J.Walsh 2016). researchers have concluded that the 3 strikes laws had lessened crime, however, I would challenge that with the fact that California, between 1977-1998, prison population grew by 500%. (J.Simone 2014). The California rate went from 88 in 1977 to 478 in 2009. This was considered the highest swing in history. (J.Simone 2014) Their prison population went from 20,000 in 1977, to a little over 100,000 in 1990, and nearly 160,000 by 2003. The 3 strikes law was created in 1993, if California's population was over 100,000 in 1990, they would arrest 6, 666 people per year. From 1990-2003, they arrested and imprisoned 5,000. Statistically the number had dropped, but the increase in detained immigrants increased. This time was also the period when drug rehabilitation began to take off. Even with the prison population dropping by close to 2000 arrestees, detainment centers, and drug rehabilitation facilities began to supplement the growing prison population. As early as 1980, reports of crack use were appearing in Los Angeles, San Diego, Houston and the Caribbean. (Marvell, T. B., & Moody, C. E. (2001)

Crack Epidemic The biggest surge in the use of the drug occurred during the "crack epidemic," between 1984 and 1990, when the drug spread across American cities. The crack epidemic dramatically increased the number of Americans addicted to cocaine. In 1985, the number of people who admitted using cocaine on a routine basis increased from 4.2 million to 5.8 million. Crack cocaine has negatively impacted the African American community in a multitude of ways. African Americans, particularly in the inner cities of the United States, have experienced alarmingly high rates of imprisonment, violence, child neglect, and HIV/AIDS transmission due to their involvement with crack cocaine. The crack epidemic, along with the AIDS epidemic increased violence in the inner city due to criminal behavior used to obtain the drug.(DAVIS,2012)Crack cocaine flooded the California streets in the 1980's. As the drugs flooded the streets, California created a sweltering 22 prison increase from 1980-2000. The three strikes laws were systematically created to respond to the increase in inner city crime due to social injustice by way of unemployment. As crime rose on the west coast, and gangs began to spiral up everywhere, the drug trade brought about black on black violence along with the drug epidemic. The elements were socially constructed to utilize the 13th amendment for the benefit of the rich.

Southern states adopted the law, and soon their prison population increased, as well as the labor for inmates. Southern states then began to use their own discretion within the laws, and in 1996 Georgia adopted the 2-strike law. Under this law, more blacks were sentenced under the 2 strikes law then white, and Latino. The three strikes laws displayed the most blatant form of prejudice within the judicial system. In California county, black population makes up 6.53% percent of the total population, but has 44% of three strikers from that county. In Los Angeles county, blacks make up 9 % of the total population, but represent 44% of the three strikers. (S. Ehlers 2004).

The racial biases associated with laws were really displayed when prosecutors and judges were given the discretion to determine whether to implement the three strikes or not. The biasness is displayed because as a prosecutor sits back and uses discretion, then years later the numbers are as present, this displays that the prosecutors were biased in their judgment and a political element must have been the motivating factor. The over compensation of blacks in comparison to Latino to white is the biggest problem within the law, when Latino gangs are, and were as prevalent as the black gangs.

Establishing lifetime workers

The racism that was socially constructed through the three strikes laws was an underhanded plot to establish a caste system and ignite free labor. By designing the three strikes laws, and giving people life behind it, would only subject them to work in prison details that are outsourced to private prison for profit. The longer the sentence, the more work you get out of each inmate. The Clinton crime bill would help speed the process, in my theory, once the Clinton crime bill was implemented; we watch 85% laws become an issue. Within the federal system, inmates are to serve 85% of the prison sentence, and still receive 3-5 years' probation. States began to adopt the 85% method, and blacks began to be overcompensated with that law as well. So instead of receiving life on your 3rd strike, under the 85% law, you could receive 30 years for your first offense, and do 85% of the time. The three strikes laws were supposedly created to decrease violent crime, then why the need for the Clinton crime bill? As the prison population increased based on these two policies, the process of mass incarceration began, leaving us at present with the most people locked up in the world, over 2 million. In response to mass incarceration, the privatization of prisons and outsourcing jobs to prisoners that should be provided to civilians. The same jobs that blacks receive living productively, were now part of the prison system. In New Jersey alone, Essex county doesn't have a DPW, which is the department of works, which are responsible for cleaning the highways, local parks, etc. Instead of paying civilians, Essex county uses Northern State prisoners to do the job. Most prisoners at this jail are 85% offenders. This job, if it was done by civilians, would pay between 40-45 thousand a year, with about 80 employees. However, prisoners do these jobs for 1.32 a day, and only 20 of them are doing the job. The privatization of prison, Clinton crime bill, and three strike laws were all constructed to utilize the 13th amendment, through law. Clinton crime bill also militarized the police, and from this militarized mind set came, stop and frisk, and racial profiling came in . The inner working of the war on drugs was constructed and seen out through a few presidencies before it would reveal, which presently brings us to the conclusion of this socially constructed plot, and that mass incarceration.

Chapter 37

The money power preys on the nation in times of peace, and conspires against it in times of adversity. It is more despotic than monarchy, more insolent than autocracy, more selfish than bureaucracy. It denounces, as public enemies, all who question its methods or throw light upon its crimes.

Abraham Lincoln

Within the policy, people that have been convicted under the three strikes laws should have their cases evaluated for biasness. The policy should be abolished due to it is only a way to implement the 13th amendment for the economic benefit of private prison, and federal prison. Within the policy, the racial discrimination utilized by the judicial system should be changed, and the discretion shouldn't be left up to the prosecutor and judge. The three strikes law was a disaster and effected black and Latino more so then any other group. The racial disparities displayed within the law were horrendous, and as blatantly direct as possible. The war on drugs began the campaign for social and political injustice against minorities, and African Americans. The American economic was established on the backs of slaves, and since slavery was abolished, political advocates utilized the criminal justice system to re-establish the same concepts of slavery. The war on drugs, and policies created from it was none other than a plot to utilize the 13th amendment to their benefit. The years 1993-1996 America not only created the Clinton crime bill, and three strikes laws, it also created deportation, and detainment of immigrants. The jail and confinement of minorities and immigrants were strategically utilized for the beneficial gain of politicians. Each of these policies displaced families, took mothers and fathers from children at the most precious times of their lives. The response of this was the future increase and conformity to gangs. The increase in gangs grew in Latino and black population causing laws to strike, and police forces to use racial discrepancies that criminalized minorities. Through this process, not only was the social climate becoming detrimental, the disparities were high, and police brutality was condoned due to the media criminalizing blacks and Latino's, making the rest of the world prejudiced towards blacks and Mexicans mainly.

Chapter 38

No nation could preserve its freedom in the midst of continual warfare.

James Madison

Before the war on drugs, President Johnson had initiated the war on poverty. The war on poverty was the nation's response to the increase in poverty across the board. With Kennedy being assassinated, we watched the economic plan Kennedy looked to establish become history. Johnson believed military aid was more important than economic aid. The poverty within America began to rise based off several factors. The war in Vietnam, and the money spent to destroy Laos, Cambodia, and Vietnam, placed the American economy in a rough position. Depending on your class level, the effect is determined. The rich remained rich, and the poor that depended on government assistance were cut short. During the 60's, America was transfixed by the war. The War on Poverty is the unofficial name for legislation first introduced by United States President Lyndon B. Johnson during his State of the Union address on Wednesday, January 8, 1964. This legislation was proposed by Johnson in response to a national poverty rate of around nineteen percent. The speech led the United States Congress to pass the Economic Opportunity Act, which established the Office of Economic Opportunity (OEO) to administer the local application of federal funds targeted against poverty.(The Economics of Poverty: An American Paradox, Prentice-Hall, 1965.) The war on poverty was set forth to eliminate poverty, Expand educational opportunities, Increase the safety net for the poor and unemployed, and increase the health and financial needs of the elderly. This was initiated by the economic act of 1964. With the war on poverty came welfare, and public housing, and assistance. The effect of the war on poverty caused more problems than good ones for future purposes. Today, black men are on child support more than any other group. Large percentage of black men that are on child support have criminal records. The war on poverty began in the 50's and resonated in the 60's. through these policies gave birth to welfare and child support. Child support has been around but the 50's and 60's began to criminalize it. Some women began to use this service as lifelong

assistance, furthermore, placing fathers in predicament they were unable to get out of.

1950: Social Security Act Amendment 42 U.S.C. § 602(a)(11) The Federal government

began requiring state welfare agencies to notify law enforcement officials when providing

Aid to Families with Dependent Children (AFDC) – a program that later became known as

"welfare" and is currently called Temporary Assistance to Needy Families (TANF) – to any

victim of parental abandonment. The purpose of this amendment was to force parents to be

accountable for providing for their children, to relieve the state – and the taxpayers – of that

responsibility. To this day, custodial parents applying for government assistance are asked

to provide information about the location of the other parent for this purpose.

For the man on child support, and with a criminal record, he is placed in a social dilemma.

With a criminal record he is unable to obtain certain values that are needed to survive

within society. Most felons are highly discriminated against, therefore the felon with

child support has more issues to deal with. Most that are on child support are in the rear

for money added while incarcerated. Men on child support are subjected to their wages

garnished, and their entire tax return being taken. This in return discourages men from

working, and most go back to what they do now. The policies created more detrimental

factors within the black household than any other, the reason being, black was socially

disadvantaged from political racist policies that placed black at the bottom of the

social hierarchy. Now the split was being implemented between men and women. With

unemployment up, and crime increasing, black men were being imprisoned faster than any

other group. This factor contributed to women needing assistance due to no male support.

Some men chose not to take care of their children which led to women placing them on

child support. In lieu of that, there is also a percentage that utilize the system and child

support as income, creating the wedge between men and their children. Judicial laws are

geared toward women in most cases related to issues regarding children, therefore men that

do not possess the finances to meet the court needs, will eventually be in the rears with child support. This then subjects men to jail time. the war on drugs, and the war on poverty assisted in dividing the black family.

The war on drugs implemented laws that directly target young black men, furthermore, distancing the black family. With some women utilizing the system as their source of income, this created more distance within the family structure for their own selfish needs. We watched men become less and less active with their children, furthermore perpetuating gang affiliation, and black on black crime. These laws and policies contributed to the systemic racism that existed with black codes, and Jim crow laws. Through the above laws black were not only subjected to the condition of these laws, they were also now part of the caste system.

Chapter 39

capitalism

It's very contradictory for a man to teach about the murder in corporate capitalism, to isolate and expose the murderes behind it, to instruct that these madmen are completely without stops, are licentious, totally depraved — and then not make adequate preparations to defend himself from the madman's attack. Either they don't really believe their own spiel or they harbor some sort of subconscious death wish

George Jackson

Capitalism is defined as, an economic system in which investment in and ownership of the means of production, distribution, and exchange of wealth is made and maintained chiefly by private individuals or corporations, especially as contrasted to cooperatively or state-owned means of wealth. "The characteristic feature of modern capitalism is mass production of goods destined for consumption by the masses. The result is a tendency towards a continuous improvement in the average standard of living, a progressing enrichment of the many. Capitalism deproletarianizes the "common man" and elevates him to the rank of a "bourgeois."(Ludwig von mises2008). The result is a tendency towards a continuous improvement in the average standard of living, a progressing enrichment of the many. Many black identify with the above statement based on impoverished situations where money is scarce. This mentality is developed through media depiction, and social influence. The flip side to most people's situation is a better financial situation. Unfortunately for blacks to develop a capitalistic mentality only placing them in the worst predicaments, some financially, and others psychologically. Capitalism wasn't designed for blacks, just look at how it is defined, an economic system in which investment in and ownership of the means of production, distribution, and exchange of wealth is made and maintained chiefly by private individuals or corporations, especially as contrasted to cooperatively or state-owned means of wealth.

CRIME & REASON: A BLACK CHOICE

Capitalism is designed and was created to suit as stated, private individuals, and corporations. Meaning that the families that participated in establishing capitalism are the families that are in control of the economics of America. Capitalism is the element that keeps the rich, rich, and the poor, poor. Individuals that represent poverty in America will oppress its own by means of capitalistic mentality that derived from social influence. America oppressed the people of the land in order to form the capitalistic system. This system was derived by the most powerful and educated men of that time. The uneducated whites became the overseers and were also manipulated by psychological and religious factors that classified blacks as inhumane. The uneducated whites that were mainly overseers inflicted the fear in blacks through physical demoralization. The system worked as the following, the uneducated whites monitored the slaves who maybe lived just above them conditionally, the blacks did the work, and the masters an government benefitted financially. The crimes that established capitalism is robbery, which was inflicted on the Indians, murder, which was inflicted on blacks that didn't obey, and Indians that rebelled, home invasion, Europeans invaded the homes of Indians and Africans and took their most valuable possession, and damage the most important element to life, family. Violence, 85% of the time is motivated by greater factors that revolve around finances. The birth of capitalism was established by the presenting factor. Most countries, in order to establish strength to compete with other countries, oppress the poor to assist them in economically becoming relevant. This mentality became the same mentality that developed the mindset of black youth. Media depiction entered the households and all the youth were able to see where things they parents could not afford.

Chapter 40

Part 1: Psychological Perspectives & Social Norms

Psychological principles contribute to how people of the world interpret it. This interpretation becomes social norms in different environments, resulting in different social climates. Different climates create different environments. Social interpretation comes by way of religion, politics, and capitalism. When the said subjects are implemented, this takes the human perspective into a cultural perspective. Cultural perspectives welcome differences of opinion based on cultural perspectives that differentiate, and this formulate politics. Politics are governed by capitalism which affects social conditions and administers the system of social stratification. Money plus power equals success. The system of social stratification is none other than a modern form of separation. This separation is done off financial status, and within each financial bracket has its own elements of prejudice, discrimination, and racism. This shows that capitalistic gains do assist in changing the social condition, but not the psychological conditioning, basically showing that social inequality and injustices are on all levels, leaving financial gains as not the problem. If finances are not the answers to what most believe poverty is the reason behind the black situation, then what is. That leaves us to focus on the mental procession of individuals of different cultures that affect the development of a culture. The psychological effect that affects the black community is the lack of identification and understanding in so many words, blacks lack a point of origin. With no understanding and no purpose, the mentality of a person will stay secluded to the environment in which he or she comes from. The environment we come from was socially constructed through a history of 200 years. The psychological interpretation of the social world to blacks is constructed around discrimination and prejudice. Looking at the world from this lens, establish the innate inferiority complex. This innate inferiority complex causes one to lack the esteem needed to succeed in the world.

CRIME & REASON: A BLACK CHOICE

The psychological component that blacks are faced with at present is the onset of a multitude of social situations that would cause detriment at present. Understand the aspect of what is at the root of black issues within America; one must identify with the family setting. The traditional family, which consists of two parents, and nuclear families. These family settings contributed to the success of black families. Analyzing historical facts, black families were at 85% two parents in 1925, and 95% in 1910. The products of these homes produced scholars, educators, and some of black major contributors to black consciousness. This was the result of two parent homes. Between 1920 and 1960, black homes went from 85% to 76%. From 1965-1991, black homes went from 76% two parent homes, to 67% single parent homes, and 54% of the children were born to teenage mothers. The black family structure is the number one issue today. Society is defined by its social institutes, a cultural group, or ethnic group success is based on how well they do within social institutes. These institutes consist of family, economics, religion, education, and state. Most ethnic, or cultural groups that have a positive advancement within the economic system, have a strong infrastructure within the rest. Looking at each of the social institutes, the family is important, it sets the tone for the rest.

Chapter 41

Looking within black family structure, we have come to identify with the dismantlement of the family. Family structures that were once two parents were now run by predominantly women, and men were nonexistent. This affected the daughters as well as the sons within the home. Immaturity has been the root of child birth within black communities. When I say immaturity, it's based on the rate of teenage pregnancies to already broken homes. In most cases, the result of teenage pregnancy comes by way of neglect within the child's developmental stages. The immaturity lies within two teenagers, both from single parent homes conceiving children. The root of this was at an all-time high in 1991. Teenagers conceiving children, who are both from single parent homes, lack the necessary needs to raise, and support a child. This I believe comes because most children that come from these homes have emotional deprivation syndrome. Emotional Deprivation Disorder is a syndrome which results from a lack of authentic affirmation and emotional strengthening in one's life. A person may have been criticized, ignored; neglected, abused, or emotionally rejected by primary caregivers early in life, resulting in that individual's stunted emotional growth. However, we will look at the black population in total in order to determine the present conditions. To understand the black situation, along with the social institute, they created genres for blacks to be identified as. This in return, affects the total population. Blacks as a whole have been systematically, and emotionally depriving the just humanistic right. Looking at criticism, one can see how blacks have been represented in the critic's eyes. Blacks have been looked down upon based on their skin complexion, criticized for being 3/5th of human, lazy, un ambitious, uneducated, low self-esteem, and violent. The world has criticized blacks to where It has a direct effect on their self-esteem. With media, and social influence, criticism in a negative way will have an emotional effect on a group as a whole, furthermore causing emotional deprivation. Ignored, black issues have been ignored since the turn of the century. Issues that cause an emotional response affect blacks. With social injustice, and social inequality being ignored, this in return affects the social institution. Racist policies that govern the USA, affect blacks socially, and economically, causing a dysfunction within the developmental community. These policies have ignored blacks, furthermore, affecting a group as a whole. Based on neglect, blacks have been neglecting human rights, and have also been neglecting advancement in certain career fields. With political issues, and social issues neglected that aid in the betterment of a group, this form of emotional deprivation causes one to lack motivation, and ambition. Abuse, abuse for blacks comes by way of 400 years. The abuse is the most detrimental because there is a psychological and physical base that can affect someone emotionally. From the beginning of slavery, the physical and psychological abuse was embedded in religion, one reason; whites utilized the bible to justify slavery. This form of psychological abuse caused blacks to believe that their place in the world was at the foot of the white man. Black endured abuse from whippings, watching their husband killed and beaten, their wives killed, and raped, as well as their children taking from them. Psychologically to live with that, along with the physical abuse, this problem would trickle down into generation creating an innate inferiority. As the years moved on and out of slavery, blacks now faced physical abuse by way of the KKK, black legions, and white families who took it upon themselves to lynch and kill blacks. The psychological response is to always live in fear of the possibility of being attacked by one of the above. Abuse for blacks followed them throughout the century, and we would see this same abuse by police, and law enforcement agencies. Blacks killed during slavery, killed during the KKK era, and now at the hands-on police officers. Through this systematic cycle of violence, white America was able to establish an innate superiority within their group, and an innate inferiority within blacks. Looking at the above, they played a major part in the dismantlement of the black families. Blackman were killed before their times by the hands of police officers, and the KKK, leaving homes fatherless. Black leaders were socially destroyed by the media, or killed by law enforcement. the racist political system that neglect and ignored the violence that were being done to black, affected them psychologically, they had no answer or help to stop these murders. The sense of feeling hopeless, and unable to fight for your family psychologically caused stressor within the communities.

Chapter 42

social institutes that govern the world

Looking at the social institutes that govern the world, the systemic racism that exists within each affected the black community. Through the process, and social injustice and inequality, black began to develop strategies to oppress and discriminate against their own. From 1965-1980, the social environment of the black community went into a state of social dilemma.

A social dilemma is a situation in which an individual profits from selfishness unless everyone chooses the selfish alternative, in which case the whole group loses. The drug trade and gang culture were the first stage to the social dilemma within the black communities. The gang culture gave birth to neighborhoods becoming territories. The violation of these particular territories would end up in death. The once unified group from the 60's would be divided in the 70's. from 19651970, black communities fell economically due to the riots.

The fall of the job market within these communities caused black to struggle financially. Within these communities, the struggle that was already present through years of racial discrimination and racist political policies established from the 1800's . The riots were a direct response to social pressure one feels from inequality. The stress that is involved with poverty, social injustice, and equal opportunity within economics placed a great deal of strain and stress on the black man because he was unable to take care of his family as needed. Within this time frame of the 60's and 70's, there was another element that would bring despair, and added stress to black communities. Black soldiers were making their way back from the Vietnam war, only to be faced with traumatic stress, and oppressive white police officers controlling the communities. For a black man to come home from the war, for a country he fought for, only to be looked at as a second-class citizen. Psychologically this affected men, and they would develop a hate for the American government that they felt left them for dead. The homes within black communities began to pummel. Multitudes of black men that came home from the war, did not receive psychological support for mental issues related to the war. Many came home with addiction, coincidentally when the war ends, is when the drugs began to flood the inner cities. Black male that came home with addiction would soon be the addicts within the community. Also during the 70's, liquor stores began to pop up throughout the communities. During this time, an onset of mental issues began to plague the inner cities. To understand the social element that created the social dilemma, we have to look at the progression over time that led to it. Blacks by the 70's had begun to feel hopeless. This hopeless sense came from years of deferred dreams, and repeated history of it. The pressure of those deferred dreams, and constant devaluing of black America, black began to socially, psychological, and physically destroy the environments they were supposed to build upon. The first stage of destroying the communities, which was the riots, in my opinion is an act of cowardice. The fear that is embedded within the black community kept them from attacking police officers, instead they went in and destroyed their own business, and the property tax in these areas went up, forcing businesses to relocate. As businesses fled, unemployment soared, and the drug trade flourished. The flourishing drug trade gave way to domestic terrorism. This form of terrorism was inflicted on the communities, and the people within these communities were forced to withstand their homes, and environments destroyed by the kids that were raised in the environment. The blocks that were organized and supported each other during the 50's and the 60's were now split. The split eventually led to black on black crime, which perpetuated through the years. When we look at most cases involving black on black crime, it's usually related financially, robbery, or drug deals gone bad. The oppression that was implied on black by white America was now being inflicted on one another. From years of abuse, deferred dreams, and inequality. The pressure eventually had to be released, and the community is where they released their oppression and destruction. As multiple social elements invaded the inner city, the social influence shifted. As the 50's and 60's went out, the social influences of those era's also faded. The once positive social influence administered throughout the inner city, was now a negative one socially constructed through racist political strategies and policies. Before the 60's, the social influence was being educated, and intelligent, from the 70's on, drugs, gangs, and materialism. The social constructed elements eventually dismantled the moral and value system that blacks stood on. The principles were now surrounded around the capital, and blacks began to hurt their own to obtain it. The identification with the moral and value system going out the window, is looking at the identity shift. During the 60's, blacks embraced their blackness through naturalness. By the time the 80's came in, blacks began to become influenced by the media, and in due time, the mentality would shift, and black became more materialistic. This materialistic outlook took away from the principalities of the 60's. Years of economic inequality, and constant struggle, the drug trade became a new source of income. By the 80's, the collectivistic culture that blacks identified with, was now an individualistic culture.

Chapter 43

Individualistic Vs collectivistic culture

Individualistic culture is a society which is characterized by individualism, which is the prioritization, or emphasis, of the individual over the entire group. Individualistic cultures are oriented around the self, being independent instead of identifying with a group mentality. They see each other as only loosely linked, and value personal goals over group interests. Individualistic cultures tend to have a more diverse population and are characterized with emphasis on personal achievements, and a rational assessment of both the beneficial and detrimental aspects of relationships with others. Individualistic cultures have such unique aspects of communication as being a low power distance culture and having a low-context communication style. Collectivistic cultures emphasize the needs and goals of the group as a whole over the needs and desires of each individual. In such cultures, relationships with other members of the group and the interconnectedness between people play a central role in each person's identity. Within the black community, the cultural perspective drifted from a collectivistic, to individualistic perspective. The formulation of individualism affected black community, because it caused a separation amongst one another. The separation from one another began to establish a negative stance amongst each other. The history of the black race in America is defined from a collectivistic culture. During slavery, the foundation of god, and family was all they had. Families prayed, and worshiped together. Up from slavery, the establishment of collectivistic culture began to evolve; the perspective of the whole group was the same, and the goal was the same. From years of oppression and slavery, black new all they had were family, and they prided on that. Studies have shown that collectivistic cultures develop a holistic cognitive style, which is reflected in processes such as memory, visual perception, attribution style, and categorization schemas. This effect has been replicated extensively by independent research groups, supporting its robustness. (Masuda, T., & Nisbett, R. E. (2001) collectivistic culture benefit families best because they are two parent homes most of the time. Up until the 50's, the collectivistic culture stayed relevant within the black community.

By the 60's, the collectivistic culture began to crumble, and the individualistic culture began to take place. The perspective came by way of difference of opinion from different groups that began to arise during this time. Within the black community everyone that spoke felt as though they had the answers to the condition of blacks at present. The birth of the black power movement created a revolutionary stance with no action plan. Leader had a difference of opinion that divided the youth for the future to come. The black power movement crippled the black community for years to come. No action was ever met, and all the movement did was establish new prisons, stricter laws, and justifiable police brutality and killing of black men.

The more blacks felt hopeless, the more they began to develop an individualistic view of life. As struggle hit in the 70's, the drug epidemic gave some the independence, as well as the ability to take care of their family. As the social environment worsened, the violence increased with the drug traffic. The more drugs that flooded the black communities, the more black men became involved in the drug trade, the more they felt financial freedom, and economic chance. The drug trade progressed the mindset from demeans of survival. The independent mindset began to invade the black population, and we then began to go from collectivistic, to individualistic group, or way of thinking ferred to opportunity. Opportunities became wrapped **in drug sales.**

Chapter 44

Multitude of social groups /rap music gangs /individualistic culture.

The split within black home resulted in different social perspectives under one roof. Not only were there different social perspectives, there was social influence governing the individualistic culture. Within black household by the 80's, the Christian foundation that set the infrastructure within the home was now broken. When black population had 85% conformity to Christianity, the family perspectives were wrapped around the same common goal. This is the definition of a collectivistic culture, one common goal, and one perspective wrapped in the same morals and values. This established the support element that was present from the 60's and before. By time the 60's roared in, the homes began to denounce their Christian roots, and began culturally accepting different social views. The Martin and Malcolm era was the birth of the split. Malcolm criticized and attacked the religion, leaving the children within black homes to rebel. As sub groups began to take shape, blacks began to conform to different religious and political viewsAn example is, within a black family by 1995, it would be possible to have family members that are Christian, Muslim, blood, Crip, or any organization such as Black Panther, and BLA. Different views from different family members create individualistic cultures within a family. An example can be a family that consists of Christians, Muslims, 5%, and bloods. We know that Muslims and Christian have religious debates and are constantly attacking one another. Muslims and Christian don't agree with 5% calling themselves GOD. This in return causes constant debate and disagreement. Muslim and Christian wouldn't agree with 5 percenter's, Muslims, Christians, and 5 percenters don't agree with bloods. This is detrimental to family progression. The family has no principles to stand on, and the foundational perspective is divided. By the 80's black made up over 20 subgroups. These groups consist of bloods, crips, Muslims, nation of Islam, 5 per centers, Christian, Israelites, moors, and an abundance of more gangs that were popping up in the south, and Chicago. With black families dividing at the root between different religions, and sub groups, the separation of thought is now diminishing. Thoughts are now individualized for independent benefits or religious and sub group laws that one must adhere by. The dismantlement of the family structure from this perspective can cause a deeper split, if members are adamant about their belief. In some cases, family members may stop attending family functions together because belief systems are different, and parents fear the influence that may affect their children. Let's analyze this view and see just how detrimental it becomes to a culture. When we look at all other cultures, like Chinese, Indian, or any ethnic group that has a strong cultural perspective. Strong cultural values are important for family development. The family development is wrapped around one common goal. When a family, or culture of people are wrapped into different ideologies, the individualistic perspective takes ordinance, which breeds selfishness.(Nosheen, A., Riaz, M. N., Malik N. I.,Yasmin, H., & Malik, S. (2017)

The selfish perspective that governed the black community brought about separation amongst blacks. This separation in return created violence amongst one another. Looking at the multitude of social perspectives being implemented, also taking into account the multitude of socially influenced sub-groups, the separation would become detrimental, and deadly. When a culture becomes separated at the core, which is at the infrastructure of the family, the detriment will cause dysfunction within family, and onset future behavior unbecoming to social standards. Social standards began to change, and the influence was depicted through the media. This level of influence would be dire, and calamitous. In the process of this social dilemma, an influx of southern blacks began to migrate east. (By the mid-twentieth century, however, the situation had changed dramatically. Roughly 20 % of southern-born blacks lived outside their region of birth, with an overwhelming share of those migrants located in a handful of northern and western cities such as Chicago, Los Angeles, New York, Detroit, and Philadelphia (White et al. 2005). The migration brought forth clutter environments. Within the process of the migration, black communities were feeling the back draft of the riots which affected the communities more so then we like to identify. The migration mixed with the social dilemma, created frustration within black communities. This frustration was a result of socially constructed implementation of social oppression exercised by the federal governments, and politics. The political formation was taking place as black became more displaced. The larger inner cities were becoming overpopulated.

Let's analyze exactly what's taking place.

Blacks are migrating to larger inner cities by the thousands. Property value is down, unemployment is up, Overpopulation and lack of jobs are an issue. This along with the social injustice and inequality that blacks were already forced to deal with, only doubled the stress level collectively as a whole. This dilemma that took place in the 70's and 80's affected the group. Looking at the contributing factors, it's possible that high levels of depression were brewing within the communities. Lack of vital resources leads to depression. Which consist of being placed at a social disability. Social disability is defined as, being socially denied access to proper social and financial opportunities. (K.Middlemass2015)The social institutes which are designed with disadvantages to minorities, contribute to the increase in social stress. With minorities lacking finances, and government funding scarce, the drug trade would become a main source of income.

Chapter 45

Socially Constructed Environments Began to Ignite Social Stress That Later Contributed To Mental Disorders.

The individualistic mentality at this time was coming from social stress that eventually would be inflicted on the community. Drug usage and dealing became the means of income. As the drugs flooded the community, blacks began to use it to their advantage. The demand for drugs within the inner city became a necessity. The success that was depicted in the media, drugs had now given blacks hope. Drugs gave people financial freedom. Drugs became a means of survival for the addict and the dealer. As the crack epidemic hit, this made the drugs more available to youth and teens. The money made during this time was utilized in the house to take care of siblings, and parents. Young boys that were part of fatherless homes gravitated to the drug trade to assist in the home. Crack became an inner-city drug, which would eventually affect the total population in years to follow. Addicts that used the drug would soon hit rock bottom and lose all they had. Victims of the drugs began to steal and rob to obtain the drug. With crack hitting the communities, we watch crime shoot up. The black communities now were occupied by drug addicts and dealers that patrolled the streets day in and out. Liquor stores, and corner stores became designated areas of drug dealing. These areas soon became territorial demands with laws attached to them. Each block within the black community was occupied by different dealers, mainly ones who grew up on that block. The territorial aspect was designed to protect the drug sales, and establish guidelines for, in order to maintain the peace. An interruption into this agreement would result in gun fire, and violence Black on black crime spiraled in the 80's, was this a result of the crack epidemic, or the social injustice that was being inflicted on blacks. Is it possible to be a result of both? Can one be a contributing factor for the other? Individualism became more prevalent as blacks began to indulge in socially constructed crimes. With the drug trade came two new occupations, robbery, and home invasion. As the drug trade flourished and blacks began to make money and invest in materialism, an underground element was formed, and created a resource of the drug dealers, which was robbery and home invasion. Inner cities produced individuals who chose not to invest in the day-to-day drug dealing, they chose to lie in wait for the dealers to make the money, then rob them, or enter the house with demands. Some of these cases result in death, normally black on black crime. The drug trade brought on the violent temperament that would on-set black on black crime. The 80's gave birth to this mentality, and rap music would spread and perpetuate it.

While blacks indulged in this new found resource, the government constructed a capitalization off the new found resources. This capitalization would be the increase in prison systems, along with privatized prisons. During the 80's, the war on drugs campaign administered by the Reagan administration would soon give birth to laws that affected blacks. The incarceration rate in the 80's soared as blacks began to indulge in the drug trade. With black men going to jail during the 80's brings us to the statistic discussed earlier. Black families by 1991 were now 67% single parent homes, and 54% of those single parent homes were teenage mothers. Was this a result of the soaring drug trade, and new prison policies? My theory is, when looking at statistical facts, we know that black families were 76% two parent homes in 1965, and in 26 years, bringing us to 1991, where black families were 67% single parent and 54% were teenage mothers. The drug trade helped dismantle the black family, in connection with all the social elements that took place during the 60's. The drug trade gave birth to a new genre of rap music. The one conscious rap produced by the likes of KRS1, public enemy and so forth was now replaced with onyx, and MOP, along with a slew of music which promoted the same message. The music gave blacks another opportunity at success. Everyone desired to be a rapper, or a sports figure. The psychology of this is, white America utilized black America's talent and creation, and established an economic system of wealth for themselves. This is evident when we look at the owners of sports franchises record companies. In sociology, this is defined as the exploitation theory. The exploitation theory is the theory, most associated with Marxists, that profit is the result of the exploitation of wage earners by their employers. It rests on the labor theory of value which claims that value is intrinsic in a product according to the amount of labor that has been spent on producing the product. (Karl Marx, Capital, Vol. 1) Thus the value of a product is created by the workers who made that product and reflected in its finished price. The income from this finished price is then divided between labor, capital, and expenses on raw materials. The wages received by workers do not reflect the full value of their work, because some of that value is taken by the employer in the form of profit. Therefore, "making a profit" essentially means taking away from the workers some of the value that results from their labor. This is what is known as capitalist exploitation. (Jon Elster, "Exploring Exploitation", The Journal of Peace Research, Vol. 15, No. 1, pp. 3-17)Music, sports, and comedy are examples of the exploitation of blacks. They were means of opportunity created to establish white wealth and demonize blacks. This is seen more so within the music and being labeled gangsta rap. This demonization that's created by the media, which is also owned by the record labels, and sports franchise owners, are in support of the prison system, which are possibly supported by the same owners. This in return gives a clear exploitation of blacks.

Chapter 46

Separation Amongst the Group

Media influence depicted resources that were needed to be socially involved with the world.

Blacks from these large cities had no way to obtain resources needed to sustain life at present. Media increased the social dilemma that was plaguing the communities. The need for success began to affect the collectivistic home fronts that were once prevalent. With drugs, and so called gangs rising at the same time, this would increase the separation even more. Blocks that were occupied by gangs, began to get involved into the drug trade. The drug trade increased the separation, and individualistic mentality. Drug dealing gave individuals independence that they so long yearned for. . As the years passed, black on black crime became more prevalent, and in the larger inner cities this would become an epidemic. The west coast was affected most by black on black crime. This was by way of drugs, and gangs. Crack hit the west coast first in south central, and began to spread throughout the entire coast. The spread of drugs and gangs would increase territorial demands, gangs controlled the Los Angeles streets, and in return terrorized their own neighborhoods. By the 90's, the influence within the black communities were controlled by multiple different schools of thought. There were a substantial number of gangs, religious organizations, religions, and sub-groups. The separation consisted of separation from the way of thinking, with black population making up multiple sub-groups, this changed the way of thinking, and this way of thinking would soon clash with other ways of thinking. An example of this would be Christian VS Muslim perspective, or blood VS crip, or 5% VS nation of Islam. There are other groups that bash the other for the purpose of establishing their way of thought as factual. The first form of separation came by way of Dubois, and Booker T Washington, blacks chose to pick a perspective, however the Dubois and Booker T debate and clash wasn't as detrimental to the consciousness of blacks. Next came the Malcolm X, and Martin Luther King clash. This was the most detrimental because it attacked the

204

religion, and all blacks had to put faith in was their religion. As Malcolm attacked the

religion, the separation would be more detrimental than that of Dubois and Booker T. The

religious aspect that Malcolm attacked caused the split to affect the home front. This split

would come between the generations. Blacks were used to the religion and Christian roots

that were embedded in them. Malcolm attacked that, and caused the children of these homes

to second guess the religion their parents had brought them up on. That was the first crucial

blow to the family, difference in opinion, and constant ridicule of one's belief. Next came

the many black power movement groups. Again, differences in opinion, and thought lead to

disagreements, and violence. This was seen at the UCLA campus when John Huggins and

Bunchy Carter were killed by members of the Ron Karenga organization. There was much

black power movement rising from 1963-1969. The next wave of separation would come by

1969-1975, when all gangs came into play. By 1975, black communities consisted of gang

members, Christian, and Muslims. From 1975-1990, multiple sub-group rose based on the

drug trade, increasing the separation within black communities.

To separate a group at the conscious level of thought, or level of intellect, affect the group.

With more followers than leaders, the conformity will be high due to lack of leadership

by most. With the rise of sub- groups, each had a perspective which they seemed was

the right perspective for blacks in America. When a group didn't agree with the others'

perspective, they bashed them publicly and behind the scenes. (Diesendruck, G., Chiang,

W.-C., Ferera, M., & Benozio, A. (2019). This bashing led to violent temperaments and spat

public spats. The one thing to look at is how white America publicized all clashes within

the black population. Media and news reporters glorified, and constantly made public notes

to Martin and Malcolm differences. Media publicized this for the sole purpose to gain

the most attention possible. The opposite ideologies, and codes that blacks lived by, made

their actions justifiable. Example, it would be easier for a Crip to kill a blood, because

they have opposite ideologies, no matter if they are the same people from the same ethnic

background. The difference in thought, and oath, separates them, and in this separation, violence against one another is the outcome. Socially the inner cities were becoming more prone to black on black crime the capitalistic mentality that create America was now being operated within the communities. The only difference, whites inflicted this level of oppression on blacks, blacks were now implementing these same measures on one another. The violent behavior used to inflict pain and suffrage on blacks in the past, was now being used on each other. Through years of psychological oppression implemented within the social institutes, the lack of adequate funds, and access to wealth, along with the social development into an individualistic culture, blacks violence toward one another was a product of social construction. From being socially denied adequate means, or an income to provide beyond just food, blacks between 1950-1990, were at a severe poverty level. This poverty level took a toll on the mentality of blacks.

Crime, is it free will, or is it socially constructed? Free will is defined as; the power of acting without the constraint of necessity or fate; the ability to act at one's own discretion. Crime is defined as; an action or omission that constitutes an offense that may be prosecuted by the state and is punishable by law. If crime isn't free will, is it nature versus nurture, of pure survival? Survival is instinctive, and motivated from an internal drive. Criminal behavior has internal properties that activate when homeostasis is off balance. Those internal drives relate to hunger, and the energy system. Hunger is a motivation for all crimes to be committed. Other properties that increase a person drive to obtain are materialism that is socially accepted. This is the process of capitalism that America has been built off. Poverty affects the internal drive, the lack of necessities ignite criminal behavior. Criminal behavior is classified by: drugs, violence, robbery, burglary, theft, murder, rape, etc. crime is impulsive, and premeditated, but is it still free will. Hunger can have anyone impulsive or violent. In the judgment and reasoning of criminal behavior, the means to obtain a resource can be life or death. Criminal behavior for black males is socially constructed through systematic policies and laws. The internal drive to commit crime is socially constructed through social stratification, socioeconomic status and social hierarchy. Socioeconomic status- is an economic and sociological combined total measure of a person's work experience and of an individual's or family's economic and social position in relation to others, based on household income, earners' education, and occupation are examined, as well as combined income, whereas for an individual's SES only their own attributes are assessed. However, SES is more commonly used to depict an economic difference in society as a whole. Social stratification is a kind of social differentiation whereby a society groups people into socioeconomic strata, based upon their occupation and income, wealth and social status, or derived power (social and political). As such, stratification is the relative social position of persons within a social group, category, geographic region, or social unit.

In modern Western societies, social stratification typically is distinguished as three social classes: (i) the upper class, (ii) the middle class, and (iii) the lower class; in turn, each class can be subdivided into strata, e.g. the upper-stratum, the middle-stratum, and the lower stratum (Saunders, Peter (1990) These titles place people in categories, the minorities are at the lower spectrum of the hierarchy. Being at the lower end leaves you at the helm of discrimination, poverty, inequality, social injustice, and financial strains. Living within urban areas, some families have suffered from the above for generations. The generational problem with families is the mentality becomes embedded within the cultural perspective, and eventually becomes the social norms. This concept is like one has accepted their fate without putting an effort to change the past mentality. Lack of any of the above can result in criminal behavior. Blacks have been on the lower spectrum of society for hundreds of years. Within this spectrum developed criminal behavior that was devised to make ends meet.

The birth of the drug trade during the 80's more so the crack epidemic escalated criminal behavior. Crack became a resource to blacks, and others. With crack came robbery, home invasion, and other crimes that were plotted against the drug dealers. The escalation in drug sales only became worse. Neighborhoods became territories. The behavior amongst the inner city was that of survival. The instinct of survival or nature versus nurture was triggered by internal motives. Youth watched as their homes went without food or proper clothing for years. Children in black families endure these issues as early as 4 years old, and progress into the teen years. The social perception of that child will be fueled with anger, and the need to obtain the things he or she didn't receive in the home. what that child environment provides, he or she will utilize to make money to take care of home and feed themselves. The boys from the home either began, selling drugs, committing robberies, or stealing car or from stores. Each of the crimes committed or based on survival instinct, and a need to suppress an internal drive. Do you believe the child that indulges in this behavior is aware of the consequences? I believe not, they only see the money made and the void filled. The environment was created for blacks to subject themselves to criminal behavior, with the purpose of growing the prison industry. The growth of the prison industry is to establish cheap labor based of the 13th amendment. The same ideologies that establish slavery, and Jim crow, created a caste system out of black families. A caste system is a class structure that is determined by birth. Loosely, it means that in some societies, if your parents are poor, you're going to be poor, too. Same goes for being rich, if you're a glass-half-full person. This is the definition of a caste system. The title such as socioeconomic status and social stratification brings about a caste system. These caste systems perpetuate criminal behavior, due to poor and poverty-stricken environments. Political strategies are devised to create future behavior. Social perception, and social cognition, define the process of thought that exists within a person's psychological interpretation. How one sees the world, through these concepts, will develop their social perception around their said environment.

Criminal behavior as it is defined, becomes the process of one's thinking, with the reason behind the behavior being justified in their eyes. All acts of crime have a reason. Crime is committed with reason, and those reasons are surrounded by needs, and wants, internal driven motives with a financial incentive. Even in acts of impulse, the thought patterns that lead up to the decision to commit the act, goes through a process before the act. In impulsive acts, there is a lack of rationale, and emotion are the internal driver, which has biases that may cause one to commit an act that they will regret. Even so, the act took a thought process before it reacted. Within criminal behavior, the committed act always has reason, and within that reason, one arrives at a choice. That choice is based on a slew of factors, finances, food, eviction, etc. traumatic stressor creates emotional response, and acts of impulse take course. Still, the choice lies in the hands of the subject committing the act. Within the black community, mainly large cities and neighboring cities, most families are suffering from one of the above, and there is a strong chance that the father isn't present. These issues lead to future behavior, and in those future behavior created the most detrimental factor of them all, black on black crime. (According to FBI data, 4,906 black people murdered other blacks in 2010 and 2011. That is 1,460 more black Americans killed by other blacks in two years than were lynched from 1882 to 1968, according to the Tuskegee Institute.) (https://www. jefferymyersunleashed.io/black on black by the numbers")"University of Toledo criminologist Dr. Richard R. Johnson examined the latest crime data from the FBI's Supplementary Homicide Reports and Centers for Disease Control and found that an average of 4,472 black men were killed by other black men annually between Jan. 1, 2009, and Dec. 31, 2012." Black males were more vulnerable to violent victimization than black females. Younger blacks were generally more likely than older blacks to be victims of violence. Blacks who had never married were more likely than all other blacks to be victims of violence • Blacks in households with lower annual incomes were at a greater risk of violence than those in households with higher annual incomes. Blacks living in urban areas were more likely than those in suburban or rural areas to be victims of violence. https://www.bjs. gov/content/pub/pdf/bvvc.pdf Within three years of release, about two-thirds (67.8 percent) of released prisoners were rearrested. Within five years of release, about three-quarters (76.6 percent) of released prisoners were rearrested. Apr 9, 2018 The most frequently listed prior convictions were property crimes, closely followed by drug crimes. Drug crimes had a recidivism rate of 62.7%. Other felonies had the highest recidivism rate at 74.2%, followed closely by property crimes at 66.4% (44%) prisoners released in 2005 were arrested at least once during their first year after release. About 1 in 3 (34%) were arrested during their third year after release, and nearly 1 in 4 (24%)were arrested during their ninth year. (Mariel Alper, Ph.D., and Matthew R. Durose.)In 2014, African Americans constituted 2.3 million, or 34%, of the total 6.8 million correctional population. African Americans are incarcerated at more than 5 times the rate of whites. The imprisonment rate for African American women is twice that of white women. Nationwide, African American children represent 32% of children who are arrested, 42% of children who are detained, and 52% of children whose cases are judicially waived to criminal court. Though African Americans and Hispanics make up approximately 32% of the US population, they comprised 56% of all incarcerated people in 2015. If African Americans and Hispanics were incarcerated at the same rates as whites, prison and jail populations would decline by almost 40%

Schuetze, S. (2013). Ill fated: the disease of racism in Julia Collins's The Curse of Caste. Legacy: 2. A Journal of American Women Writers, (1), 82. Retrieved from 3. http://ezproxy.montclair.edu:2048/login?url=http://search.ebscohost.com/login. aspx?direct=true&db=ed sglr&AN=edsgcl.336178105&site=eds-live&scope=site

Dovidio, J. F., Gaertner, S. L., & Saguy, T. (2015). Color-Blindness and Commonality. American Behavioral Scientist, 59(11), 1518–1538. https://doi-org.ezproxy.montclair. edu/10.1177/0002764215580591

Henry, J., Dionne, G., Viding, E., Petitclerc, A., Feng, B., Vitaro, F., … Boivin, M. (2018). A longitudinal twin study of callous-unemotional traits during childhood. Journal of Abnormal Psychology, 127(4), 374–384. https://doi-org.ezproxy.montclair.edu/10.1037/ abn0000349.supp (Supplemental

Paradies, Y. (2006). A systematic review of empirical research on self-reported racism and health. Retrieved from http://ezproxy.montclair.edu:2048/login?url=http://search.ebscohost. com/login.aspx?dir ect=true&db=edsuph&AN=edsuph.786&site=eds-live&scope=site

Seale, 1970, part I; Newton, 1973, parts 2–3; Bloom and Martin, 2013, chapter 1; Murch, 2010, part II and chapter 5.

Ture, Kwame; Hamilton, Charles V. (1992). Black Power: the Politics of Liberation in America. New York: Vintage Books. p. 114

Muhammad, Tynetta. "Nation of Islam History". Retrieved April 17, 2014.

Austin, Curtis J. (2006). Up Against the Wall: Violence in the Making and Unmaking of the Black Panther Party. University of Arkansas Press

The Iran-Contra Affair 20 Years On. The National Security Archive (George Washington University), 2006-11-24

Lawrence E. Walsh, "Firewall: The Iran-Contra Conspiracy and Cover-up" (New York: Norton & Company, 1997) p. 290 et. seq.

Zinn, Howard (2003), pp. 587–58

Tower, John; Muskie, Edmund; Scowcroft, Brent (26 February 1987). Report of the President's Special Review Board (Report). Washington: U.S. Government Printing Office. Retrieved 20 January 2019.

Webb, Gary (1998). Dark Alliance: The CIA, the Contras, and the Crack Cocaine Explosion. New York: Seven Stories Press. ISBN 1-888363-68-1.

Zinn, Howard (2003). A People's History of the United States. New York:

James Calvin Hemphill, "John Schreiner Reynolds", Men of Mark in South Carolina: Ideals of American Life Vol. II; Washington, D.C.: Men of Mark Publishing Co., 1908.

Kermit L. Hall, "Political Power and Constitutional Legitimacy: The South Carolina Ku Klux Klan Trials" Archived 2013-03-16 at the Wayback Machine; Emory Law Journal 33, Fall 1984.

D. Alan Heslop:Political system/Encyclopædia Britannica March 17, 2017

URL:https://www.britannica.com/topic/political-system/The-functions-of-government

Burlingame, Michael. "Abraham Lincoln: Domestic Affairs". Charlottesville, Virginia: Miller Center of Public Affairs, University of Virginia. Retrieved April 14, 2018.

Whittington, Keith E. (March 2000). "Bill Clinton Was No Andrew Johnson: Comparing Two Impeachments" (PDF). Journal of Constitutional Law. Philadelphia, Pennsylvania: University of Pennsylvania. 2 (2): 422–465. Retrieved April 14, 2018.

Printed in the United States
by Baker & Taylor Publisher Services